SURVIVE!

Written by Guy Campbell
with Dominique Enright, Juliana Foster, Guy Macdonald,
Steve Martin, Martin Oliver, Lottie Stride and Tracey Turner

Illustrated by Simon Ecob
with David Shephard, Stuart Taylor and Katy Jackson

Edited by Lauren Farnsworth,
Amanda Barnes, Rachel Carter, Hannah Cohen,
Sally Pilkington, Liz Scoggins and Jen Wainwright

Cover design by John Bigwood

SURVIVE!

-→HOW TO SURVIVE←-- ANYTHING, ANYWHERE

Buster Books

First published in Great Britain in 2013 by Buster Books, an imprint of
Michael O'Mara Books Limited, 9 Lion Yard, Tremadoc Road,
London SW4 7NQ

The material in this book was taken from nine titles previously published
by Buster Books: *The Boys' Book One*, *The Boys' Book Two*, *The Boys'
Book Three*, *The Boys' Book of Adventure*, *The Boys' Book Of Spycraft*,
The Boys' Book of Survival, *The Girls' Book One*, *The Girls' Book Three* and
The Time-Travellers' Handbook.

 www.busterbooks.co.uk

 Buster Children's Books

 @BusterBooks

Text and illustrations copyright © Buster Books 2006, 2007, 2008, 2009 and 2013
Additional illustrations from www.shutterstock.com

A CIP catalogue record for this book is available from the British Library.

ISBN: 978-1-78055-178-4

2 4 6 8 10 9 7 5 3 1

Printed and bound in September 2013 by CPI Group (UK) Ltd,
108 Beddington Lane, Croydon, CR0 4YY, United Kingdom.

Papers used by Michael O'Mara Books are natural, recyclable products
made from wood grown in sustainable forests. The manufacturing processes
conform to the environmental regulations of the country of origin.

Contents

9 How To Survive

10 How To Make Your Own Survival Pack

12 How To Survive A Shark Attack

14 How To Light A Fire

18 How To Survive A Volcanic Eruption

20 How To Build A Survival Shelter

22 How To Ride Whitewater Rapids

26 How To Escape From A Burning House

28 How To Create A Quick Disguise

30 How To Tackle A Tyrannosaurus Rex

32 How To Repair A Spacecraft

34 How To Dress A Wound

36 How To Survive A Shoal Of Piranhas

38 How To Get Out Of Being Tied Up

42 How To Be A Good Leader

44 How To Parachute

46 How To Vanquish A Vampire

48 How To Escape From The Belly Of A Whale

50 How To Survive Radiation

52 How To Survive On A Desert Island

56 How To Bring An Aircraft Down In An Emergency

61 How To Find The North Star

62 How To Treat Stings

64 How To Survive A Visit From An Abominable Snowman

66 How To Climb A Rope To Safety

68 How To Survive An Avalanche

72 How To Handle A Meat-Eating Plant

74 How To Escape From Quicksand

76 How To Survive The *Titanic*

78 How To Put Someone In The Recovery Position

80 How To Tame A Lion

82 How To Build A Camouflaged Den

86 How To Choose A Good Place To Shelter

88 How To Fight Off A Crocodile

90 How To Make Fresh Water From Sea Water

92 How To Set Up An Advance Warning System

94 How To Fight With The Samurai

96 How To Recognize Deadly Snakes

101 How To Survive A Snake Bite

104 How To Avoid Lightning Strikes

106 How To Escape A Capsizing Ship

110 How To Survive An Earthquake

112 How To Defend A Medieval Castle

114 How To Bust A Ghost

116 How To Make A Simple Raft

120 How To Make Your Escape

122 How To Survive A Tornado

SURVIVE!

126 How To Survive
A Zombie Invasion

130 How To Get Home
Using Nature's Clues

134 How To Carry
Someone To Safety

136 How To Survive The
Bubonic Plague

138 How To Survive At Sea

142 How To Survive
An Arctic Adventure

146 How To Avoid Being
Chomped By A Hippo

148 How To Survive
A Swarm Of Angry
Honeybees

150 How To Survive A Rip
Current

152 How To Throw
An Opponent

154 How To Find Your Way
In A Maze

156 How To Survive
In Bear Country

158 How To Survive
In The Desert

162 How To Survive
An Alien Encounter

164 How To Cross
A Rope Bridge

168 How To Escape The
Clutches Of A Boa
Constrictor

170 How To Make An
Underwater Escape

172 How To Make A Camp
In The Wilderness

175 How To Read
A Compass

176 How To Put Out The
Great Fire Of London

178 How To Make
A Swift Exit

180 How To Survive A Flood

184 How To Survive In
A Horror Movie

186 How To Build An Igloo

190 How To Track Animals

How To Survive

Life is about more than homework and cleaning your room. The world can be a dangerous place, full of wild animals, untamed nature and cunning enemies. With this book you will find you can survive anything, whether it's an avalanche, a snakebite or a sinking ship.

Survival also means playing it safe. The techniques in this book are for use only in emergencies. Take a responsible adult with you if you go on an expedition, because it is never a good idea to undertake any of the activities described alone.

We urge you at all times to make yourself aware of and obey all laws, regulations and local byelaws and respect all rights, including the rights of landowners, and all relevant laws protecting animals and plants and controlling the carrying and use of implements such as catapults and knives.

Above all, exercise common sense, particularly when fire or sharp objects are involved, and follow at all times safety precautions and advice from responsible adults. That said, it is fun to learn new skills, and they may one day be useful.

How To Make Your Own Survival Pack

The equipment you take with you will depend on the type of expedition you are planning. But whether you are camping in the wilderness, hiking through mountains or trekking through jungle, there are some expedition essentials that will keep you warm, dry and well fed.

BEFORE YOU LEAVE

🐾 Check that all your electrical appliances are working and fully charged, or have new batteries, before you set off.

☙ Take a 'survival bag' with you. This is a large, brightly coloured waterproof bag that you can sleep in if necessary.

☙ Pack the equipment and rations you would need to survive for at least 24 hours in an emergency.

ESSENTIAL ITEMS

- Water (as much as you can carry)
- Water purifying tablets
- Food rations (including high-energy food, such as chocolate and nuts)
- Maps
- A good compass
- Warm clothing (including a hat)
- Hiking boots
- A waterproof coat
- Camping equipment: tent, sleeping bag, cooking utensils
- A first-aid kit
- A whistle
- A flashlight (with spare bulb and batteries)
- A pocket knife with a selection of heads
- A waterproof sheet 1.5m by 2m
- A wristwatch
- Sturdy plastic bags for carrying water
- Fish hooks and twine
- A mobile phone
- Waterproof matches, a lighter and tinder
- A magnifying glass (can be used to start a fire)
- A candle
- At least 8m of cord
- Wire for making snares
- Insect repellent
- Sunscreen
- An emergency blanket.

HOW TO SURVIVE A SHARK ATTACK

While the danger of being attacked is hugely exaggerated in many movies (you are statistically more likely to be killed by a hippopotamus than a shark), you should still take these precautions to minimize your chances of becoming a shark snack.

DOS AND DON'TS

🐾 DO stay away from fishing boats and groups of sea birds where sharks are likely to be hunting.

🐾 DO get out of the water immediately if you cut yourself. Sharks can smell blood from a long way off and will soon come to investigate.

🐾 DO try to swim with a group of people. Sharks are less likely to attack if they are outnumbered.

☙ DO wear dark, plain colours. Brightly coloured bathing costumes or wetsuits, and even shiny watches and jewellery, may make you look like a tasty exotic fish.

☙ DON'T provoke a shark by lunging at it or waving your arms and legs around. If a shark feels threatened, it is much more likely to attack.

ACTION IF ATTACKED

If a shark has decided to attack, it will begin darting to and fro, zig-zagging and lifting its head. Here's what to do:

☙ Swim away as quickly as you can and get out of the water. If you can't, stay calm. Don't thrash and splash about.

☙ Try to get into a position where your back is protected by rocks, a reef, or by another swimmer. That way you can defend yourself from the front.

☙ When the shark attacks, hit it with a sharp object or your fists. Aim your blows at its eyes, gills or the end of its nose, which are its most sensitive areas.

If you're in a group form a circle facing out. Shout underwater, kicking and punching outwards at the same time.

How To Light A Fire

There are a several ways of making fire if you don't have any matches or a lighter. The 'fire-bow drill' is a clever version of the 'rubbing two sticks together' method.

HERE'S HOW TO DO IT

1. Collect some 'tinder'. Tinder is anything that catches fire very easily, such as dry, thin grass, cotton fluff and feathers. You need a good handful to start your fire.

2. Find a wooden stick for your bow. It needs to be a strong stick that is about 60cm long and about 1cm wide. It must be quite stiff, but still flexible. A thin bamboo cane is good for this.

3. Now you need some cord or string. A bootlace is perfect if it is long enough. Carefully carve a slight notch around each end of the bow. Attach the cord to the bow at either end around the notches. The cord should be stretched tightly enough to make the bow bend slightly.

4. The drill should be a piece of hard, dry branch about 30cm long and 2.5cm wide. It should have a sharp point at one end and be rounded and blunt at the other. The straighter your drill, the easier it

will be to use. Twist the drill into your cord (see the picture below).

5. Make a base called a 'fireboard'. You will need a flat piece of soft, dry wood, 2.5cm thick, 15cm wide and 60cm long.

6. Carve a v-shaped notch in one end of the board about 2cm deep and 2cm wide, as shown below. Put your tinder in the notch.

7. Make a hole in the board that is about the same width as your drill and 1.5cm deep. The hole should be centred near the notch you made.

8. Find a stone with a natural hollow in it, about the same size as the blunt end of your fire drill. Push the blunt end of your drill in the stone's hollow and rest the sharp end in the hole on your board. Alternatively, make a hole in a piece of hardwood that fits in your hand and use that instead of the stone.

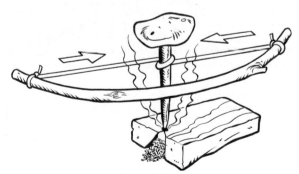

9. Kneel on one knee and place your other foot firmly on the fireboard. Push down lightly on the stone with one hand and hold the bow in your other. Pull the bow back and forth. Begin slowly, and keep a steady pace. Spin the drill until wood dust and smoke start to come out of the hole.

Hold your bow horizontally and your drill vertically. A pinch of sand in the hole under the drill will create more friction, and therefore more heat.

10. When you see smoke coming out of the hole push and pull the bow faster and harder. The wood dust will fall into your notch and on to your tinder. When smoke starts to come from your pile of tinder, you have made a 'coal'. Gently blow on the smoke to produce a flame.

11. Now you have a little fire, you can add some small sticks, followed by some bigger ones until your flame looks stronger. You can then build your campfire around it using larger pieces of wood.

SURVIVAL SKILL WARNINGS

It is extremely dangerous to start a fire. Always follow the advice below when starting a fire in a survival situation:

🐾 Keep a container of water or soil at hand in case you need put out your fire quickly.

🐾 Choose a suitable spot for your fire, away from anything that could catch alight, such as trees, bushes, dry grass and buildings.

🐾 Make sure that all your belongings are right out of the way and remove any stones from the area – they could get really hot and shatter.

🐾 Always keep an eye on the fire to make sure it does not get out of control. When you have finished, make sure you put the fire out and that no embers are left glowing.

How To Survive
A Volcanic Eruption

First of all, know what you are up against. Below the surface of the Earth, a build-up of gases and the movement of the crustal plates can increase pressure to a point where it can no longer be contained. The result is an explosion of boiling lava (molten rock), flaming gases and red-hot fragments of rock and dust. Pretty scary stuff.

🐾 At any given time there are usually at least 12 volcanoes erupting somewhere in the world. If you live near one make sure you are prepared.

🐾 Stock up on provisions of bottled water, food, medical supplies, blankets, warm clothing and batteries in case power lines are cut. Collect water in your bath, sinks and containers as mains supplies may quickly become polluted.

🐾 In the event of an eruption, seek shelter at home and don't leave unless advised to by the authorities. Keep listening to the radio or TV for news and advice.

🐾 If you go outside, wear a mask and goggles to keep volcanic ash out of your eyes and lungs.

Keep gutters and roofs clear of settling ash, which could bring down the house upon you.

🐾 If possible, don't wander away from other people, and always remain on the trodden paths.

🐾 If you are caught outside during an eruption, be aware of the hazards that come with an eruption: the flying debris, hot gases, lava flows, explosions, mudslides, avalanches, boiling water sprays from geysers, and floods. If you are in an area that could experience a lava flow, be ready to outrun it and never try to cross it.

🐾 Look for hills and head towards them. They may afford you some protection from the destructive and devastating effects of the eruption.

How To Build
A Survival Shelter

This easy survival shelter can be made in a couple of hours. It will keep you warm and dry, and help you get a good night's sleep, which is vital in preserving your strength and maintaining a positive attitude.

1. Find two strong, straight sticks, each with a fork at one end. Make sure they are the same length (about 1.2m). Sharpen the unforked ends and dig them firmly into the ground to a depth of at least 40cm, and 2m apart. If one stick is longer than the other, dig it further into the ground to even up the height.

2. Find another long, straight stick over 2m long and rest this in the forks of the upright sticks. This is your 'ridge pole'. Secure it to the forked sticks with twine.

3. If you have a tarpaulin throw it over the ridge pole to make a tent. If it is large enough, use some of the tarpaulin to form a floor for you to make your bed on.

4. Peg the tarpaulin down with sticks, or place heavy stones along the wall edges to keep it secure.

AN ALTERNATIVE SHELTER

If you don't have a tarpaulin, make a shelter by building two walls out of branches and poles.

1. Find a long pole (about one and a half times as high as the tallest person using the shelter). Find a tree with a forked branch to support your shelter at one end.

2. Place the pole against the tree, then place smaller poles each side of the main pole to make a sloping framework. Next, weave some thin, bendy branches through the small poles to make a criss-cross frame. (See image **A**.)

3. Cover your frame with materials such as dead leaves, dry ferns, moss and grass. Add some light branches to the outside of the shelter to stop your insulating material blowing away. (See image **B**.) Then spread a thick layer of dry grass on the floor of the shelter for you to lie on.

How To Ride Whitewater Rapids

River-rafting can be a great adventure. If you are lucky, the river will start out calm, so you are able to paddle along smoothly. But when things change, and you can hear the water crashing around rocks and thundering downhill, you'll feel very glad that you are wearing a life jacket and more importantly a helmet – water can really get wild!

SAFTEY GEAR

The correct safety wear is essential for whitewater rafting. You'll need to wear a life jacket. The jacket will stop your back and shoulders from being bruised, as well as keeping you afloat. You must also wear a crash helmet.

RIDE THOSE RAPIDS

The rider with the most experience is seated at the back of the large rubber boat. He uses his paddle as a rudder to steer the boat through the rapids, avoiding obstacles in the water. It's up to you and the other rafters to paddle with all your might and keep your boat moving along the safest course.

RAPID-RIDING RULES

To ride whitewater rapids to safety, follow these essential rapid-riding rules:

- Teamwork is very important. If you don't work together, your boat will tip over and you will end up in the water.

- Pay attention to your leader's instructions at all times.

- Keep a firm grip on your paddle. Keep one hand over the top of the paddle (called the T-grip) for extra control. This will also make sure you don't whack your fellow riders on the head with your paddle as you stroke through the water.

* Don't sit straight and rigid in the boat. By relaxing your posture and letting your body move with the boat, you're more likely to stay in your seat for the whole ride.

* Try and steer the boat towards patches of calmer water, called 'eddies'. These are formed when the water swirls behind large obstacles in the river, like rocks or logs, and will help you to get your breath back before you tackle the next big drop.

* If you find yourself going for an unexpected swim, don't panic and don't let go of your paddle. Try to swim back to the boat so that the others can pull you back in.

* If the water is flowing too fast and you can't swim against it, lie on your back and float down the river feet-first until the boat catches up with you.

WARNING. Riding rapids is extremely dangerous and not something you should do by yourself. However, there are organized whitewater rafting trips where you can enjoy the experience in safety.

How To Escape From A Burning House

H ouse fires are rare but deadly. Insist that your home has smoke alarms fitted on each floor. Check their batteries are working once a week and never let anyone take the batteries to use in other appliances. Make sure that everyone in your household knows exactly what to do in an emergency. Here are some useful tips.

FIRE!

* As soon as you become aware that there is smoke in the house, make sure everyone is awake and ready to get out of the building quickly. Do not stop to take anything with you.

* If you can get out through a door, touch it with the back of your hand before opening it. If it is cool, it's probably safe to go through. Turn your face away then open it a crack to make sure. Smoke and fumes rise, making the air near the floor easier to breathe, so crawl through on your hands and knees. Once you're through, shut the door behind you. This can slow down the progress of a fire by as much as ten minutes.

🐾 If the door is hot when you touch it, take an
alternative route to safety. If you're heading out
through a window and need to break the glass,
cover it with a sheet, a towel or a pillow. Protect
your hand and arm with fabric as well. Smash
all the glass out of the frame so you don't cut
yourself climbing through.

🐾 If you are trapped in a room with running water,
soak tea towels, curtains, pillowcases or blankets
in water and stuff them into the cracks under the
doors. This will stop smoke seeping into the room.

🐾 Dial the emergency services as soon as possible,
then let the professionals do their job. Once you
are outside, get as far away from the building as
possible and check everyone is out.

How To Create A Quick Disguise

Y our spy kit should contain at least one item that can be used if you realize you are being tailed at any point on a mission. It should be something that will instantly change your appearance, and will not be out of place in any situation.

A HAT
This should be a hat you can tuck easily into your pocket, so you can put it on or take it off whenever you need to. Don't choose a jester-style ski hat – it would be too eye-catching. A good spy hat should be easy to pull down over your hair and eyes.

SUNGLASSES
On a warm, sunny day, what could be more normal than wearing sunglasses? Slip on some shades to look instantly incognito. Not only will you disguise your identity, you'll also

make it harder for other people to see exactly where you are looking, putting you at an advantage.

A SCARF

Keep a scarf in your bag to wrap around your neck at a moment's notice. A dark, plain scarf is better than brightly coloured checks. You don't want to stick out.

> Never use sunglasses as a disguise indoors, or during the winter months – you are more likely to draw attention to yourself.

LAYERS

Several thin layers of clothing, such as a couple of differently coloured T-shirts, a thin sweater, a hooded top and a light coat, give you lots of options for changing your appearance on a mission. Put whatever layers you are not wearing in a rucksack, or change the order of the layers to give you a completely different appearance.

REVERSIBLE CLOTHES

Keep a lookout for reversible clothing – for example, this could be a coat that is bright red, but when worn inside-out is dark blue. This is a super-simple way to change your identity. When spotted, just duck out of sight for a quick change and vanish into the crowd.

HOW TO TACKLE A TYRANNOSAURUS REX

To minimize your chances of ending up as a T. rex's lunch, here are some life-saving precautions to take should you ever find yourself in prehistoric times.

DOS

☙ DO avoid a T. rex's gnashers. His powerful jaws are lined with up to 60 teeth. Bite marks found on the fossils of other dinosaurs show that T. rex can bite off 70 kilograms of meat in one go – which is more than the whole of you!

☙ DO run for it. T. rex walks on its two powerful back legs but can't run very fast. Its maximum speed is about 18 kilometres per hour.

☙ DO look out for a dinosaur with a mouth like a duck's bill – and then stay as far away from it as you can. This is an Edmontosaurus, T. rex's favourite food.

DON'TS

🐾 DON'T hide. T. rex has good eyesight and a brilliant sense of smell. It will sniff you out quickly.

🐾 DON'T let the T. rex tread on you. A fully-grown T. rex is up to 14 metres long, 6 metres tall and weighs around 7 tonnes.

🐾 DON'T be tempted to fight. Even though, compared to its back limbs, a T. rex's front limbs are tiny, you wouldn't stand a chance. Its claws pack a powerful punch. Some dinosaur experts think T. rex used its 'arms' for holding prey – and you don't want to prove them right.

How To Repair A Spacecraft

If you ever find yourself zooming into outer space, you'll need to be able to fix anything that goes wrong with your spacecraft – after all, there are no garages in space! Read on to learn how to survive in space when your spacecraft breaks.

SPACECRAFT SURVIVAL

🐾 Always wear a spacesuit. It protects against the extreme temperatures of space that can range between 135°C to −82°C. It also provides you with oxygen to breathe. A spacesuit costs over £12 million, but it is essential kit for all astronauts.

☀ Switch on your helmet camera so that what you see is relayed back to 'mission control' – your helpful team based back on Earth.

☀ Fitted to your suit is a long thick line that is attached to your spacecraft. This line provides you with oxygen and allows you to communicate with mission control. They will be watching and instructing you on how to fix the damage.

☀ Locate the damaged area. To do this, astronauts use a gas canister to make sure they float in the right direction. To move forwards, fire the gas in the opposite direction – backwards. The force of the gas will push you forward.

☀ Move around the outside of the spacecraft very slowly. If you rush about, the spacesuit could tear on the spacecraft's sharp edges, releasing the oxygen and killing you instantly.

☀ Use tools, secured to a tool belt around your waist, to fix the damage. Tools will float off into space if they are not attached to a tool belt.

☀ Space tools are specially made so that they can be used by astronauts wearing thick gloves. You can practise your spacecraft repair skills at home by trying to fix your bike wearing thick oven gloves.

How To Dress A Wound

There aren't many adventurers who don't get injured at some point. Usually, these injuries are no more than small cuts. Small wounds needn't be a problem, as long as you are prepared and know how to dress them properly. Here's how to do it.

ESSENTIAL FIRST-AID KIT
You can't dress a wound without a first-aid kit. Below are the essential items every adventurer should carry in his or her first-aid kit – they can mean the difference between life and death.

You Will Need:
- a clean cloth
- fresh drinking water
- antiseptic cream
- sticking plasters.

WARNING. When dressing a wound, you should always get an adult to look at it first.

COMBATING INFECTION

The smallest wound can become very dangerous if it becomes infected, so the most important thing to do is clean it. Follow these steps immediately.

1. If blood is still dripping out of the wound, press a piece of clean cloth gently against the wound. Applying some pressure should soon stop the bleeding.

2. Once the bleeding has stopped, pour some drinking water over it so that any little bits of dirt are washed away. Dab the wound gently with the clean cloth to dry it.

3. After washing and drying the wound, stop it from getting infected by rubbing a small blob of antiseptic cream all over it.

4. Now you need to dress the wound to keep the dirt out. The easiest way to do this is to use a sticking plaster. Peel the paper off the back and carefully lay the padded part of the plaster over the open wound.

5. Change the plaster whenever it gets dirty or wet. Each time you change the plaster, clean the wound.

6. Check the wound regularly. If there is swelling or pus oozing out of it, if it continues to hurt, or if it doesn't appear to be healing, it may be infected and you should see a doctor as soon as possible.

How To Survive
A Shoal Of Piranhas

You might have heard that a shoal of vicious piranha fish can strip a human being to a skeleton in a matter of seconds, but this is just not true.

In reality, these toothy fish don't live up to their fearsome reputation. There are lots of different kinds of piranhas, and some are actually vegetarians. Even the most dangerous piranhas do not prey on large mammals (like you). It is true, however, that a piranha can give you a very nasty nip – in fact it could easily bite off a finger or a toe. Here are some tips on how to hang on to all your digits in piranha-infested waters.

PREVENTIVE MEASURES

🐾 Be aware of piranha habitats – they live in slow-moving rivers, streams and lakes in South America. The most dangerous type is the red-bellied piranha.

🐾 The dry season can be a dangerous time to go into the rivers of South America – prey can be in short supply, so piranhas will be peckish.

☙ Avoid water close to rubbish dumps, or trees where birds nest – these can be rich sources of food, so piranhas are more likely to lurk there.

☙ Piranhas can sense blood in the water, so don't enter the water if you have a bleeding cut anywhere on your body.

If you do see piranhas, don't panic – thrashing about will only attract them. Move calmly and smoothly through the water to the bank, where you can get out and panic in relative safety.

How To Get Out Of Being Tied Up

No matter how careful they are, all adventurers run the risk of capture. There is, however, a secret method to help you escape if your hands have been tied. If your enemy is tying you up, he will be nervous that you will break free until you are tightly bound. You can take advantage of his nerves and try to control his movements.

WARNING. Never leave someone tied up, and never tie someone up to the point where they feel uncomfortable.

Tying you up would be a highly-effective way of holding you prisoner, but only if you're tied up so well that you can't move. The most important thing for you to do while being tied up is to make sure that there is some slack or loose rope. Later on, this will enable you to move enough to reach the knots.

In order to do this, you need to work from the moment you are being tied up – every second counts. Bunch your fists and breathe in as much as possible to expand your muscles and your rib cage. Keep doing this until your rival spy has finished tying the last knot. When you relax, you should find there is a fair amount of slack in the rope. Use the extra space you have to start loosening the knots.

ESCAPE TACTICS

To practise escaping, first you will need to be tied up. Find a piece of string and ask a friend to play the role of the enemy and follow the instructions overleaf:

1. Put your left arm out so that the palm of your hand is facing upwards. Wrap the string once around and lay the string over the inside part of your wrist, as shown.

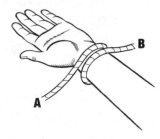

2. Wrap the string around your wrist again so it makes an X-shape, as shown.

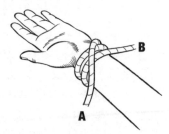

3. Put your right wrist next to your left wrist.

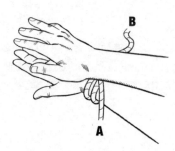

4. Flip both your wrists over, so that the string goes over your right wrist, as shown. Ask your friend to tie a tight knot in the string so your wrists are tied together.

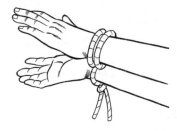

5. To escape, twist your right wrist round and the string will open up so that you can easily slip your hands out.

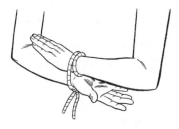

Use a thicker rope when practising escaping, as the knots will be easier to undo.

How To Be A Good Leader

There may be a time when you find yourself with a group of people in a dangerous situation. Someone needs to take the lead – and that someone could be you. Here are some things to remember if you want to step up.

MAKE A STRONG START

When you first meet the members of your team, make eye contact. It gives an excellent first impression. A confident, firm handshake helps, too. Stand upright with your shoulders back. This will give your teammates confidence in your abilities. Try to remember everyone's name and repeat it back to them as you introduce yourself: 'Hello, Jack, I'm James.' This will make people feel you're interested in them and they will be more likely to trust you.

BE GOOD AT SOMETHING

If you read this book from cover to cover, your excellent survival knowledge will be sure to impress your team. Sporting talent is impressive, but if you lack athletic prowess don't worry, metalworking and woodworking skills are really useful in survival situations, too.

If all else fails, be witty and charming. Many leaders get to the top by putting people at ease and making them laugh.

ALWAYS TRY TO REMAIN POSITIVE

* Try to see solutions to the problems that face you rather than moaning about them. Complaining wastes time and can lower your team's spirits.

* Keep any criticism to a minimum. If you're quick to praise your team when they perform a task well, they will stay keen and cooperative.

* Don't ask anyone to perform any chores that you wouldn't be happy to take on yourself.

* Making use of your team's varied talents and expertise can only get you ahead.

* Don't have favourites. Make sure everyone feels that they are a valued member of the team.

Owning the biggest and the best tools is always a plus.

How To Parachute

I magine flying deep into enemy territory. Your plane keeps low to avoid radar detection, skimming above the hills and trees below. This is a 'LALO' (Low Altitude, Low Opening) parachute jump. Give a confident thumbs-up when the pilot signals it's time for the drop, and get ready to exit the plane.

Here's what you need to remember to ensure success:

1. Push yourself out of the plane, holding your body in the arc position – chest first.

2. As you fall through the air, keep your eyes on the horizon, and count slowly to four before pulling the cord. Once the parachute opens, look up to check that the lines and canopy are not tangled. If anything is wrong, quickly pull the cutaway cord and then the reserve cord – at low altitude, there's no time to lose.

3. Steer yourself towards the landing zone, using the left and right steering lines, and looking before each turn.

4. Prepare for landing. As the ground gets closer, turn your body into the wind for the final turn. This will slow your descent and ensure you're in control of your canopy. Use your right-hand steering line to guide you, making adjustments with the left.

5. Pull on both steering lines at once to flare the canopy. As the ground rushes towards you, move your body into an arc. As soon as the balls of your feet hit the ground, you should continue falling in the direction your parachute drifts. Rest your chin on your chest and twist with your hips. This will cushion your fall as your legs give way on impact with the ground.

6. Wait for a second as the air rushes back into your lungs, then gather your thoughts. You have to get to your feet and check you have no injuries or breaks.

If you have a fellow jumper, stay alert and watch out for collisions.

HOW TO VANQUISH A VAMPIRE

Do you have suspicions about your neighbour? The one who never comes out during the day? He is thin and pale, with slicked-back hair. He has a whispery voice and when he speaks he covers his teeth. Could he have something to hide? You had better do some checking ...

1. Choose a bright sunny day to scatter garlic bulbs around his front door then retreat to a hiding place. When he comes out, watch his reaction. If he heads rapidly back indoors, you might be on to something.

2. Return with a large mirror. Stand in a hidden spot where you can see his front door reflected in the mirror. When the door opens, can you see his reflection? If not, he could be a vampire.

3. If all signs point to him being a vampire, you must take action. Arm yourself with garlic, a crucifix, a sharpened wooden stake, and a bottle of holy water (ideally a spray bottle). Collect a small group of friends, who should be similarly armed.

4. With your companions, make your way in daylight into the vampire's basement and find his coffin. Be prepared in case a werewolf or another monster comes out from the shadows to defend his master.

5. Surround the vampire with your friends. As you are so well supplied with garlic and other vampire deterrents, he should weaken rapidly. When the vampire cowers, it is time for you to strike.

6. Hold your stake firmly in your hands and aim for where the vampire's heart would be if he had one, and plunge! The vampire should crumble into dust before your eyes.

WARNING. Always triple check your suspicions before you send a vampire into eternal darkness – chances are he's just a quiet man with bad teeth!

How To Escape From The Belly Of A Whale

Although scientists agree that the mouths and bellies of some whales are big enough to swallow a human whole, it is very unlikely that you will ever find yourself inside one. This is because whales like to eat sea creatures, not humans.

However, if a whale does accidentally swallow you up, don't panic. The following instructions will help you to survive.

* There is plenty of room in a whale's stomach – it can hold nearly a tonne of fish – and hopefully enough oxygen to breathe.

* It will feel very hot because a whale's belly is surrounded by thick 'blubber' (fat) which keeps it warm in cold seas, but resist the

temptation to take off your clothes – the whale's digestive juices will react with your skin as it tries to digest you. Keep as much of your skin covered as possible.

* To avoid starving to death, try tickling the stomach or jumping up and down to give it a tummy ache to make it sick – you would then come out with the sick … nice!

* If none of this works, as a last resort use a large knife to try to cut through the thick stomach wall to freedom. Whichever way you try and escape from the belly of the whale, it won't be a pleasant experience …

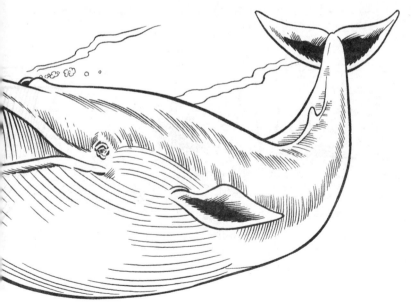

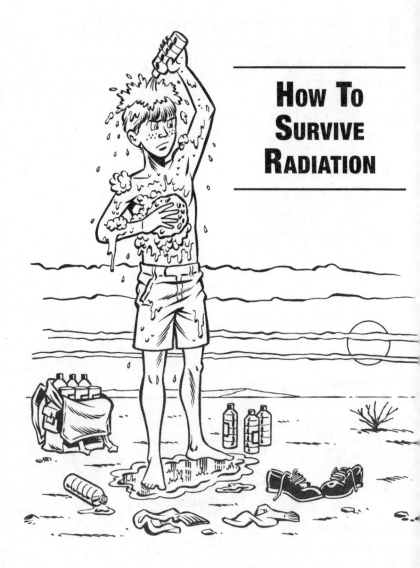

How To Survive Radiation

I f you have been lucky enough to survive a nuclear explosion you might think you're in the clear, but radioactive dust produced by the blast will settle on the ground. It will remain radioactive for months, even years after the explosion, contaminating everything around the bomb site. Radiation will make you extremely sick and can prove fatal in strong doses. Here's how you can survive it.

🐾 To avoid the radiation, you need to get moving and leave the affected area immediately. Travel as far from it as you can.

🐾 Spend as little time outside as possible. As you travel away from the affected area, shelter in buildings, preferably those made from concrete. Make your bed for the night as far inside the buildings as possible so that solid materials protect you from the air outside.

🐾 Breathing contaminated air is a hazard, but not nearly as dangerous as drinking radiated water or eating contaminated food. Stick to tinned and bottled foods until you have put a lot of distance – and that could mean 200 kilometres – between yourself and the location of the explosion.

🐾 Wash thoroughly and regularly with soap and water that has not been contaminated. Drink lots of uncontaminated water to help flush radioactive materials from your system.

HOW TO SURVIVE ON A DESERT ISLAND

H ave you ever thought about what you'd do if you were marooned on a desert island? Here's how to make the best of the situation until help arrives.

THIRSTY WORK

Nobody can survive for more than a few days without drinking water. In the heat of a desert island, you will be sweating a lot and dehydrating rapidly. Finding water is your first priority.

With luck there will be fresh water flowing on your island. Search along the shore for a stream running into the sea. Follow the stream back towards its source as far as you can. When you can go no further, check that the water is running clear and that it doesn't smell bad before you drink any. Only drink a tiny amount at first and increase day by day. This allows you to check it is safe to drink before you have consumed too much.

If you can't find a source of fresh water, you will need to collect water. There are two main methods. First, make sure you have any containers available positioned to collect rainwater when it falls. Store the water somewhere cold and shady during the day to stop it evaporating. Second, every morning you should collect the dew that has formed on the leaves of plants – this is perfect for drinking. Mop it up with a clean cloth and wring the cloth into a container.

TAKE SHELTER

It is essential to stay out of the heat of the sun on your island, so the next thing to do is make a shelter. Look for something that could form the basis of your shelter, such as a dry rocky outcrop, a fallen tree, or even a cave. Gather reeds, twigs, and large leaves and use them to finish your shelter. You could try weaving branches together. Line the shelter with dry leaves, pine needles or bracken.

FOOD

Some doctors say a human being can survive without food for four to six weeks. However, if you leave it for more than a few days you will be too weak to look for food when you need it. Why not make a fishing rod with string, a stick and a safety pin as a hook, and see if you have any luck landing a fish? Alternatively you could attempt to spear fish with a sharpened stick. Failing that, most seaweed is edible, though you might have to boil it for a while.

Coconuts are a great source of food and drink, and hopefully these will be falling from the trees on your island. The hard part is to open them.

1. Once you have removed the green outer layer, pull off the 'husk' – the hairy outer layer.

2. At one end of the coconut, you'll see three dents – like two eyes and a mouth. Hold that end in one hand. Find the 'seam' that runs between the eyes. Follow the seam to the middle of the coconut. Imagine a line running around its fattest part.

3. Find a large rock and give the coconut some hard taps along this line. Keep turning the coconut so you hit it all the way round the seam. After a few good whacks, the coconut should break into two halves.

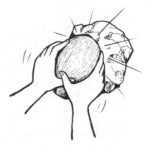

4. Scrape out the white 'meat' inside with a sharp shell or piece of rock. Smell the inside of the coconut before you eat it. If it smells sour or mouldy, throw it away.

How To Bring An Aircraft Down In An Emergency

No one likes to think about it, but if something ever happened to the pilot of a plane that left him unable to fly it, you and the rest of the passengers would be in very grave danger. Make sure you're ready to jump into the pilot's seat and save the day.

1.   Many light aircraft have autopilot (a device which, once set and engaged, automatically keeps the plane

on a preset course). This will keep the plane flying on the settings the pilot has dialled in. Even if there is no autopilot, the pilot will have 'trimmed' the aircraft to fly 'hands off'. This means that the plane will maintain a steady speed, course and height. Additionally, the pilot will have filed a flight plan, so local air-traffic control (ATC) will be aware of your flight.

2. Sit down, but don't touch the controls immediately. On the instrument panel in front of you (usually in the centre of the top row of instruments in front of the pilot) there is a device called an 'attitude indicator', also known as an 'artificial horizon' or 'gyro horizon'. This shows the position of the aircraft relative to the ground – that is, whether the wings are level, and whether the aircraft is climbing or descending, or flying at a steady height. It shows a pair of straight lines that represent the plane's wings. Behind them is a sphere or ball divided horizontally; the upper half is usually blue (for sky) and the lower half usually brown (for Earth).

Try not to panic! You will be much more able to take control if you have a clear head. Plus, remaining calm will encourage any other passengers to keep calm too.

On an attitude indicator,
these horizontal lines
represent the plane's wings.

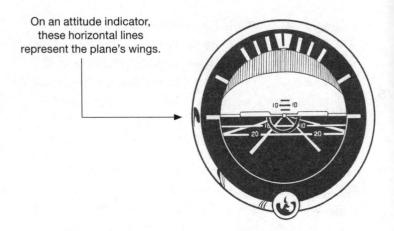

3. Check to see if the two lines on the attitude indicator representing the aircraft's wings, and the white dot between them showing the position of the aircraft's nose, line up with the fixed line on the instrument face representing the horizon. If they don't, it means the 'autopilot' is off and the plane is not following a level course.

4. If the autopilot is off, you need to level the plane. Move the yoke in front of you little by little to get the wing lines on the attitude indicator level with the line representing the horizon. Pull the yoke towards you to bring the nose of the plane up. Push it forward to bring the nose down. Move the yoke to the left and the plane will bank left, and to the right it will bank right. Do this using gentle movements of the yoke, until the plane is flying straight and level. The attitude

indicator will show the wings horizontal and the
nose of the aircraft on the line between the 'sky' and
'ground' indicators. Do not use the rudder pedals.

5. There is a radio on the instrument panel, probably
in the centre. If you can't find a microphone on the
instrument panel, take the pilot's headset. Press the
Push To Talk (PTT) button and say 'Mayday' three
times, clearly and slowly. Then say 'Pilot unconscious'.
Release the PTT button so that the person who
receives the call can talk back.

6. Below the radio is the 'transponder'. This identifies
the aircraft on radar and will send out your location
details so your plane can be tracked by ATC. Set the
dials to 7700 (or type this number in – it is the code
for 'general emergency') and ATC will know you have
a problem.

7. The controller will give step-by-step instructions how
to land the plane. Follow these carefully, but don't
hesitate to ask for things to be repeated if you are
at all unsure. Essentially, he or she will instruct you
how to bring the aircraft down to a height from which
it can be safely landed. He or she will tell you what
to do about controlling engine power, lowering the
undercarriage, and turning on to a new course. He or
she will talk you through the other instruments – such
as the altimeter (measures the aircraft's height above

the ground) and the airspeed indicator. Everything in flying is geared to height, speed, course, and attitude (the angle relative to the Earth at which the aircraft is flying), and ATC's instructions will aim to keep these four factors correct at any stage during the landing.

8. You might have to land in a field or on a road, so watch out for power lines and trees, or other obstructions, such as bridges.

9. Approach your landing place in a straight line. Just before you reach the ground, pull back slightly on the yoke to lift the nose of the aircraft. This way you'll land on the main wheels beneath the wings – as you slow, the nose wheel will come down.

10. When the plane's main wheels are on the ground, immediately reduce your speed by pulling the throttle (a big black lever between the pilot and copilot seats, or a large knob, usually black, in the lower centre of the instrument panel) right back towards you. Many light aircraft have toe brakes on the rudder pedals. If these are fitted, gently press them to bring the plane to a standstill without making it skid.

11. There may be a key, like a car's ignition key, on the instrument panel. Turn this to kill the engine, once the aircraft has come to a halt. Do what you can to help the pilot, but wait until the propeller stops turning before attempting to climb out.

How To Find The North Star

For thousands of years explorers and navigators have used the North Star (also known as Polaris) to work out their direction and latitude (their position north or south of the Equator). Here's how to find the North Star in the night sky.

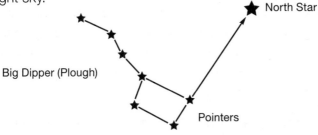

North Star

Big Dipper (Plough)

Pointers

🐾 First find the Big Dipper, which is also known as the Plough. This is the constellation which looks like a saucepan (remember that depending on where you are and what time of year it is, the Big Dipper could be upside down or on its side).

🐾 Locate the two stars that form the edge of the 'pan' furthest away from the 'handle'. These stars are often called the 'pointer' stars because they point to the North Star.

🐾 Draw an imaginary line through them. This will lead you northwards to a large, bright star: the North Star.

HOW TO TREAT STINGS

You can recognize if a person is allergic to a sting if they have difficulty breathing, their pulse speeds up, they collapse, or areas of the body away from the site of the sting swell up. If you see any of these signs, be sure to call an ambulance immediately, but also ask the person if they've got treatment with them (some carry adrenalin ready to be injected). Likewise if they've been very badly stung or have been stung in the mouth or eyes, call an ambulance at once.

Otherwise, when a person is stung, they will suffer only short-lived pain and some discomfort that can be soothed by pressing something cool on to the affected area or rubbing it with an ice cube.

BEE STINGS
If you're unlucky enough to be stung by a bee, you can follow the instructions for how to treat your sting on page 148. But if you're allergic to bee stings, always seek medical attention immediately.

WASP STINGS
Wasps don't leave their sting behind. If you dab vinegar on the stung area, it will reduce the pain.

JELLYFISH STINGS

These are painful but usually harmless (the dangerous one is the Portuguese Man-of-War, recognized by its blue-mauve bladder that floats on the surface). Rinse the sore area thoroughly. Calamine lotion will soothe it.

NETTLE STINGS

Rubbing with dock leaves (a weed with large green leaves and clusters of small greenish or reddish petal-less flowers) provides the best relief. If you can't find dock leaves try mint (recognizable by its scent).

How To Survive A Visit From An Abominable Snowman

S ome people don't actually believe that the abominable snowman (known to his friends as the 'yeti') exists, but just in case you encounter him here are some rules to follow:

1.   Never enter into a long discussion with him about whether or not you believe in yetis. This is guaranteed to make a yeti very angry. Imagine if you had trekked across a wild and desolate landscape in search of food or company only to be told that you don't exist. Wouldn't that make you abominably bad-tempered?

2.   Don't run around screaming or throwing things at the yeti. Yetis are bigger and stronger than you and if you make them cross they may attack. Stay calm and slowly back away with your arms out in front of you, your hands clearly visible and palms downwards. This will put the yeti at ease and show him that you are not about to reach for something to throw at him.

3.   Some people believe yetis are the distant cousins of human beings. So why not offer the yeti a cup of tea or some food? Snow people are often amazed by our

abominable lack of manners when receiving guests. When a yeti has guests they will always offer some wild rhododendron tea and a few snow biscuits at the very least, even if the guest was not invited.

4. Don't flash cameras in a yeti's face – snow people find this very rude. Always ask the yeti's permission before taking their photograph so they have enough time to arrange their fur in a pleasing way. If you ask the yeti nicely enough they may even let you pose in the shot with them.

How To Climb A Rope To Safety

R ope climbing is a skill that may one day save your life. Find out how to set up a safety rope that you can climb up to get out of danger.

You Will Need:
- a length of rope roughly 3m long
- a strong, healthy tree
- a stick.

1. Tie knots in the rope, about 30cm apart. Tie one end of the rope to a stick and throw it over a branch of the tree. (See image **A**.) Grab the end of the rope with the stick tied to it. Untie the stick and throw it away.

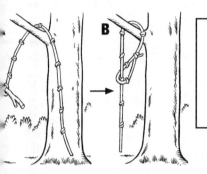

WARNING. Ask an adult to check the branch won't break when you put your weight on it.

2. Tie a loop in one end of the rope and thread the other end of the rope through it. (See image **B**.) Pull tightly on the threaded end of the rope so that the loop reaches the branch. Your rope is now ready to climb.

3. To climb up the rope, take hold of it with both hands on top of a knot at head level, bend your knees and wrap them around the rope. Rest your feet on the bottom knot. Now raise your hands up to the next knot and pull your body up. Lift your legs up until your feet reach the next knot. Repeat this until you reach the top.

4. To climb down the rope, use the knots to work your way down slowly.

How To Survive
An Avalanche

Snow avalanches occur when the snow on a mountain slope becomes so heavy that all it wants to do is travel downhill. Every year people perish under tonnes of sliding snow. So if you go skiing or snowboarding, you need to know how to avoid being caught out – especially since most avalanches are caused by the weight of a single person on unstable snow. Here are some tips:

BE PREPARED

🐾 Be alert. Before you hit the slopes, listen to the radio or TV for avalanche warnings in the area you are in.

🐾 On the slopes, look out for recent heavy snowfall and strong winds, rapid changes in temperature, cracks in the snow, and snow that sounds hollow. Avalanches are more likely to happen on steep, north-facing slopes. You might want to avoid them altogether.

🐾 Always carry a mobile phone to call for help. Keep it in a zipped pocket so it won't get damaged by snow.

- Always make sure you carry an avalanche rescue beacon. The beacon will send out a signal that rescuers can follow if you are buried in snow. Turn the beacon on when you set out on your expedition.
- Before crossing a slope, secure your snow goggles and put on your hat, gloves and a scarf. Zip up your coat and tighten the neck and cuffs. If an avalanche does happen, it will be harder for the snow to get inside your clothes.
- Choose one member of your team to make their way across the slope first. Then make sure everyone in your team crosses in the same track. Tell them to concentrate on the snow on the slope above them for any sign of movement.

EMERGENCY TACTICS

🐾 Once you spot an avalanche, you need to act fast. Don't try to outrun the snow.

🐾 Just before an avalanche hits, scream as loud as you can to warn the other members of your team, but when the snow reaches you, close your mouth so you don't swallow any.

🐾 Drop all your ski poles as they may injure you when you fall.

If you can, grab a tree or a rock to stop yourself sliding down the slope.

🐾 Avalanche snow is a bit like water. Once the snow has hit you and knocked you off your feet, try to swim through the snow. You can stay nearer the surface by swimming upwards, and this improves your chances of being rescued.

🐾 If you are unable to grab hold of a tree or rock, as the avalanche slows down, curl your body into a ball with your hands over your face. When you stop moving, quickly move your hands back and forwards to make an air space in front of your face. The snow sets hard within seconds, so this is very important.

🐾 Double-check your avalanche beacon is on. Keep calm and sit tight – help is on the way.

🐾 If you can see light, try to escape, or at least reach your hand above the surface where it can be seen. Don't waste valuable energy struggling if you aren't getting anywhere. Your avalanche beacon will be sending out signals giving your location, so remain calm and wait for help.

Spit in your breathing space and pay close attention to where this spit goes. You should be able to tell which way is up and which is down from this.

How To Handle A Meat-Eating Plant

A carnivore lives by eating meat. One of the most amazing carnivores is a Venus flytrap. Within seconds of an insect landing on this plant, its leaves snap shut. The plant then releases chemicals which dissolve the creature.

MONSTER MEAT EATERS

Nature is full of different types of meat-eating plants, with many different ways for poor little bugs to meet their doom.

Butterworts. These plants have sticky leaves. When a small insect lands on the leaf, it is trapped and covered in digestive juices.

Bladderworts. Their leaves are shaped like small bags. When a small water creature swims into one of the bags, a trapdoor springs shut, trapping it.

Corkscrews. These plants have small openings on their roots which attract tiny creatures. Fine hairs across these openings stop them from escaping.

Pitchers. These plants have folded leaves which hold digestive juices for insects to fall into.

GROW YOUR OWN MEAT-EATING PLANT

Venus flytraps grow in the wild in certain parts of the USA, but they are quite easy to grow yourself. Here's how:

1. Ask your parents to order a bulb from a supplier. Venus flytraps need a lot of air to grow, so plant it in a large bowl. Press the bulb into the soil, so that the top of the bulb is level with the top of the soil.

2. Put it in a sunny place. On winter nights, cover it with a cloth to keep it warm. Water your plant regularly.

3. Feed your plant bugs. Hold the bug with a pair of tweezers inside an open trap, so that it is touching the short hairs on the leaves. Wait until the trap snaps shut. When the trap reopens a few days later, it is ready for you to feed it again.

Don't touch the leaves of a Venus flytrap without offering it food. This will fool your plant into snapping its leaves shut, causing it to waste energy, which will shorten its life.

How To Escape
From Quicksand

Quicksand is a thick sludge that is most commonly found near beaches or rivers. In the movies people slowly sink into it until they finally disappear beneath the surface. In reality, getting stuck in quicksand doesn't mean an inevitable death. It is often only a metre deep.

BE PREPARED
Most people who perish in quicksand die by drowning. This is because quicksand is usually found in tidal areas. When the tide comes in the area is submerged under water, as is anyone stuck in the sand. The most important thing is to not to allow yourself to get stuck.

☙ If you are travelling in a team, spread out. Make sure you walk with a ten-pace gap between each team member. This way if one of you starts sinking the others can stop and help.

☙ Use a stick to prod and test the ground.

☙ Carry a length of rope that you can use to lasso nearby objects and pull yourself clear.

☙ Walk barefoot. The soles of shoes can act like a sink plunger, and will suck you down.

ESCAPING A STICKY SITUATION

☙ As soon as you start sinking, throw away any heavy objects you are carrying. You must avoid allowing your feet to plunge down into the sand under the weight of your body. Quickly lean your body backwards until you are lying flat. This will spread out your weight.

☙ Don't thrash around. Any sudden movements will stir up the quicksand and make it less stable. Wait for the sand to settle around you. Manoeuvre your walking stick underneath your hips, so you are lying across it. It will help keep you on the surface.

☙ Stay on your back, but use your arms and legs to slowly swim, crawl and drag yourself towards solid terrain.

How To Survive The *Titanic*

There's not much any one person could have done to stop the *Titanic*, a magnificent ocean liner, from sinking in the Atlantic Ocean on 15th April 1912, but here's how you could have done your best to try and save yourself.

* Get a first-class ticket. Almost all the women and children in first class survived, compared to fewer than half the women and children in third class. Most people in third class had not even been told where the lifeboats were.

- ☙ Get to a lifeboat fast – there weren't enough for all the people on board. It was recommended to have 48 lifeboats to take all the passengers, but the owners of the *Titanic* only put on 20. They didn't even completely fill the ones they launched. One lifeboat left carrying only 12 passengers.

- ☙ Tell the crewmen in charge of the lifeboats how old you are. Women and children were allowed to board the lifeboats first, so they younger you are, the better.

- ☙ Stay in your lifeboat. You may survive the ship sinking, but you won't last long in freezing water.

How To Put Someone In The Recovery Position

If you find someone unconscious, immediately call for an ambulance. If you suspect they have a neck or spine injury, do not attempt to move them unless they are in immediate danger. The recovery position is a first-aid technique that can be used on a friend who is unconscious, but is still breathing normally and who doesn't have a neck or spinal injury.

Open the patient's mouth and make sure that his airway is clear of any blockages, including his tongue. Tilt his head back and raise his chin. Check that the patient is breathing normally by looking to see if his chest is moving up and down regularly, listening at his mouth and feeling the air on your cheek. Then check that his heart is still beating by feeling for his pulse.

You are now ready to put the patient in the recovery position.

1. Gently lay the patient on his back. Kneel by his right-hand side. Take the arm nearest to you and lay it on the ground in a right angle.

2. Reach over and take the other hand and bring it across his chest. Bend the arm and place the back of the hand on the patient's cheek nearest to you, holding it there with your own hand.

3. Pull up the far (left) leg at his knee until the sole of his foot is on the ground. Then, gently bring the knee towards you (still keeping your hand and the patient's against his cheek). As his left knee comes forward, your casualty should role on to his right side.

4. Remove your hand from the patient's cheek making sure that his head is still resting on his hand. Move the leg towards the chest to form a right angle.

5. Keep the airway open by tilting the patient's head back and raising his chin. Check his breathing and pulse.

6. Keep a close eye on your teammate until help arrives, and check his breathing regularly.

How To Tame A Lion

Cats are usually affectionate animals that make great pets, but if you're planning on becoming a lion tamer you have to be a bit careful. The three vital skills a lion tamer needs are caution, bravery and patience. Here's how to teach your lion to do a trick.

JUMPING THROUGH HOOPS

🐾 It is very important that the lion trusts you. Lion tamers often raise their lions from cubs, which gives them a strong bond.

🐾 You are going to teach the lion to respond to a signal. Put a hoop in front of the lion with a toy or bright object on the other side of it. Step back and click your fingers.

🐾 At this point, the lion doesn't know what you are trying to do. If it does step through the hoop to investigate the object on the other side, reward it immediately with some food.

🐾 Keep doing this exercise, and every time the lion steps through the hoop, give a food reward. You will soon find that the lion will step through the hoop when you click your fingers even when the toy is not there.

WARNING. Remember: the 'pussy cat' you'll be dealing with is over a metre tall, weighs 200 kilograms and has teeth that could tear your head off!

How To Build A Camouflaged Den

If you're lucky enough to have a large garden or have access to an outdoor space, why not build your own all-weather, camouflaged den?

You Will Need:

- 3 bamboo canes, roughly 1.5m long
- 1 bamboo cane roughly 2m long
- a ball of string
- scissors
- large, old plastic sheeting, a groundsheet or a large bed sheet
- some heavy stones
- a trowel.

1. Decide where you want to position your den. Look for a sheltered position, out of the wind, and preferably on slightly raised ground for drainage. A good solid tree with a forked branch can form the back of your shelter, but a bush or wall works just as well.

2. Create a frame for your shelter by taking the three shorter bamboo canes and lashing them together about 15cm from the top, with a length of string, to form a tripod.

3. Place the final cane into the forks of the supporting canes to form a ridge pole. Tie it securely with string. Rest the ridge pole in the branch of a tree, then push the supporting poles into the ground at a 45° angle. Check that these supports are firmly rooted in the ground. Alternatively, rest the ridge pole securely in a bush or on top of a wall.

4. Lay the sheeting over the frame, leaving an opening at the front so that you can get in and out easily. There should be enough fabric to overlap at the front and keep out breezes.

5. Place the stones along the two edges of your sheeting that touch the ground to weigh it down and stop it blowing away in the wind.

6. Clear the ground inside your shelter of rocks, twigs and leaves so that it is comfortable to sit on. You can use a leafy branch as a makeshift broom.

7. Camouflage your den by plastering wet leaves, mud, light fallen branches or grass over the sheeting. This will also add an extra layer of insulation, making it warmer.

WARNING. Never bring a fire into your den. The fumes are extremely dangerous, as is the risk of the fire spreading.

8. Use the trowel to dig a narrow trench around the sides and back of your den. This will channel rainwater away from the inside and help to keep you dry.

9. Furnish your den with cushions or camping chairs. Sit back and get ready for your first meeting.

If you can't get hold of any bamboo, any long, straight sticks will do. Just make sure they are strong enough to take the weight of your sheeting.

HOW TO CHOOSE
A GOOD PLACE TO SHELTER

If you find yourself stranded in an unfamiliar environment, your top priority is to find a safe place to sleep. Well before darkness falls, you need to find a suitable place to shelter.

TAKE COVER

🐾 A shelter provides protection from the elements. In desert areas you will need to stay out of the sun. In mountains or polar regions rain, snow and wind will seriously threaten your survival.

☙ Caves provide good shelter. Check them out first, as you don't want to find you are sharing with a wild animal. Tell-tale signs that the cave may be occupied include bones, nests and droppings.

☙ Camping at the base of rockfaces and cliffs will offer some shelter. But if there are loose rocks lying around, these might suggest falling debris. Avoid these areas in snowy terrain, as there might be a danger of avalanches.

THE IDEAL SPOT

A clearing in a wood is the ideal spot to make camp, especially near a stream. That way you will have building materials for a shelter and water for drinking and washing.

PLACES TO AVOID

When looking for a place to set up camp here are some places to avoid:

☙ Stay away from ponds or lakes. Water that isn't flowing attracts insects that might bite you.

☙ Don't camp in a hollow at the bottom of a hill. Rain water may run off the hillside and flood your shelter.

☙ Never camp at the top of a hill as this will be exposed to the wind and rain. Your shelter could easily be blown away.

How To Fight Off A Crocodile

C rocodiles are amazingly efficient killing machines. They might seem slow, but they can move very quickly when they want to, and leap out of the water very suddenly and at great speed.

1. If you're standing near a lake and a crocodile springs from the water towards you – run as fast as you can, and keep running for at least 15m. If you cannot run, try to get up on to the creature's back and stand on its neck to stop it from opening its jaws – crocodiles have weak jaw-opening muscles and you can hold their jaws shut without too much difficulty. On the other hand, their jaw-closing muscles are incredibly powerful and it is almost impossible to prise them open.

2. Alternatively, if you are in the water and a crocodile unexpectedly surfaces, you won't be able to outswim it, but if you can grab its jaws before it opens them, you'll have a chance of keeping its jaws shut (this assumes there's no part of your body between them). Yell for help.

3. If the crocodile has clamped its jaws on one of your limbs, try to reach for a stick or anything else to use as a weapon and hit its sensitive nose repeatedly and poke it in the eyes. (A man actually managed to make a crocodile let go of his arms by biting its nose as hard as he could.) It might just back off, but crocodiles are quick and persistent, and you'll have to keep fighting until you're safe. Carry on yelling and fighting hard to get away.

4. As a last resort, play dead. Crocodiles shake their prey underwater to drown it but will stop when they think it's dead. Quickly take your chance to make your escape when it moves off.

How To Make Fresh Water From Sea Water

If you are marooned on a desert island after a shipwreck, you'll be surrounded by water. Annoyingly, you won't be able to drink any of it because it is salty. With any luck, you'll have salvaged some useful utensils, such as cooking pots and tin cans, from the wreck of the ship. Using these, here's how to make delicious fresh water from nasty brine.

1. Stand a clean, empty tin can on the bottom of an empty cooking pot or bowl. Pop a stone into the can to keep it in place.

2. Pour sea water into the pot until the level is about three quarters the height of the can. Make sure the sea water does not enter the can.

3. Put the pot's lid on upside-down, so that the lid handle is over the empty can inside. Put the pot over a campfire and wait for the water to boil.

4. As the water boils, carefully pour a little cold sea water over the lid of the pot to keep it cool. Make sure that your fire doesn't go out. As the water boils it turns to steam and leaves the salt particles behind in the pan. The steam collects on the inside of the lid and, as it cools, 'condenses' into pure water droplets. The condensation then runs down the lid's handle, dripping into the can. Keeping the outside of the lid cool with cold water makes the steam condense faster.

5. After 20 minutes use some twigs as tongs to lift the lid of the pot and check the water's progress. Once the can is almost full, very carefully remove it from the pot with the tongs. The pot, can and water will be very hot.

6. Leave the can of water to cool before drinking.

WARNING. Don't try doing this unless you have been shipwrecked. Sea water tastes disgusting and is extremely bad for you if it has not been boiled in the correct way because it contains huge amounts of salt.

How To Set Up An Advance Warning System

You can never be too careful where your bedroom is concerned. To survive snooping siblings or parents, it's vital to be prepared. A few seconds' warning may be all you have to ensure you aren't taken unawares.

PROTECT YOUR HQ

🐾 Balance an empty tin can on the door handle inside the room. Anyone trying the door will dislodge the can, warning you of a potential intruder and giving you time to conceal your secret files.

🐾 Angle a mirror so that you always have a view of the door to your room. This way no one can sneak up on you.

🐾 Keep your HQ dimly lit and the light in the corridor outside your room on. This will help you to keep an eye out for shadows under the door, created by anyone standing behind it listening.

If you have to go out and you want to know if someone has been snooping around while you are gone, you can carefully tape a single hair to the bottom of your door. Leave your door open a couple of centimetres and tape one end of the hair to the doorframe and the other to the inside of the door. If someone opens it, you'll come back to find the hair snapped in two. The only thing you have to figure out is who it was.

How To Fight With The Samurai

The 'samurai' are members of a group of ancient Japanese warriors, who ruled Japan for 700 years. Samurai warriors are considered to be some of the

greatest swordsmen in history. The warriors were a fierce and terrifying sight, clad in strange armour, with wide helmets and armed with long, curved swords.

To survive a fight with a samurai, you will have to learn the martial art Kendo, which means 'the way of the sword'. Kendo is performed with a partner – a 'motodachi'. The first part of the practice involves a special ceremony.

1. Stand opposite your motodachi, about nine paces apart. Hold your stick, called your shinai,

on your left-hand side if you are right handed, or on your right-hand side if you are left handed.

2. Lift your shinai to hip level, and take three steps forwards, towards your partner.

3. On the third step, lift your shinai up and forwards. Your partner should do exactly the same. Hold your shinai so the tips are almost touching.

4. Move your left foot so the heels of both your feet are almost touching.

5. Bend your knees and go into a deep squat, spreading your knees wide apart. This is called sonkyo.

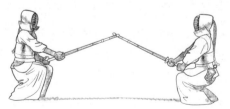

6. Stand up.

How To Recognize Deadly Snakes

I f you're travelling in an area that is known for its venomous snakes, make sure you can recognize what some experts consider the top five deadliest snakes.

THE INLAND TAIPAN (ALSO KNOWN AS THE FIERCE SNAKE)

* **Found In:** Dry, arid regions of Australia.

* **Deadly Rating: 1st.** This snake's venom is the deadliest in the world. Just one milligram of its venom is fatal to a human being.

* **Nature:** Generally inactive but will attack if provoked.

☆ **Appearance:** These snakes can grow up to 1.7 metres long. The back, sides and tail are often pale brown in colour, but the rest of the body is usually black in winter and dark brown in summer.

THE AUSTRALIAN BROWN SNAKE
(ALSO KNOWN AS THE COMMON EASTERN BROWN SNAKE)

☆ **Found In:** Australia, Indonesia and Papua New Guinea.

☆ **Deadly Rating: 2nd.** This snake is responsible for more deaths in Australia than any other.

☆ **Nature:** Aggressive.

☆ **Appearance:** These snakes can grow up to almost 2 metres long. They are mostly brown and can have a range of patterns on their backs, including multi-coloured bands and speckles. They can move very fast across the ground.

THE MALAYAN KRAIT (ALSO KNOWN AS THE BLUE KRAIT)

- 🐾 **Found In:** Southeast Asia.

- 🐾 **Deadly Rating: 3rd.** The Malayan krait's venom is 15 times stronger than a cobra's.

- 🐾 **Nature:** Timid during the day. More aggressive at night.

- 🐾 **Appearance:** This snake can grow up to 1.5 metres in length. Its back has black and white bands that widen as they reach its white underside. The head is greyish, with lighter lips. This snake will often hide its head within its coiled body for protection.

THE TIGER SNAKE

🐾 **Found In:** Southern Australia, Tasmania and its coastal islands.

🐾 **Deadly Rating: 4th**. If untreated, more than half of bites are fatal.

🐾 **Nature:** Aggressive if threatened.

🐾 **Appearance:** Tiger snakes grow to about 1.5 metres long. They often have bands, like a tiger, but range in colour from yellow and black to olive- and orange-brown with a paler underside. If threatened, tiger snakes make a loud hissing noise and will raise their heads like a cobra to strike.

THE SAW-SCALED VIPER

* **Found In:** The Middle East, Central Asia, India and surrounding areas.

* **Deadly Rating: 5th.** These vipers are responsible for more deaths than any other species of snake.

* **Nature:** Aggressive and quick-tempered.

* **Appearance:** They grow to about 1 metre long, and have short pear-shaped heads, with quite large eyes. The scales on their lower sides stick out at an angle of 45°. When threatened, they form C-shaped coils and rub their coils together, making a loud sizzling noise. They move quickly with a side-winding action.

How To Survive A Snake Bite

Not all snakes are poisonous and even poisonous snakes don't always inject venom into a victim when they bite. However, always assume a snake is poisonous, just in case.

SELF-TREATMENT

It's of utmost importance that you seek medical help immediately if you are bitten by a snake, even if you don't yet feel unwell. If you can't, remain calm. Panicking will increase your heart rate and this will help the venom spread throughout your body faster.

TAKE THE FOLLOWING PRECAUTIONS

🐾 If you've been bitten on your arm or hand, remove your watch as your hand or wrist might swell up and your watch could become painfully stuck. Remove any other pieces of tight clothing that are near the bite.

🐾 Dress the wound with a bandage that fits snugly, but not too tightly. You want to restrict the flow of blood slightly to the bitten area, but not cut off the blood supply altogether.

🐾 If you're with another member of your expedition party get them to wash your bite with soap and water.

🐾 Lie down flat so that the area of your body that was bitten is not higher than your heart. This will slow down the speed at which venom travels to this vital part of your body.

🐾 Ask your friend to tie a splint to the affected limb. This will restrict its movement and help prevent the venom from spreading around the body.

DOS AND DON'TS OF SNAKE BITES

🐾 DON'T copy what you see in the movies. The hero usually cuts across their buddy's snake bite with a knife and sucks out the poison. Don't do this. You might make yourself sick, and cutting the flesh around the bite might help the venom to spread and could cause infection.

🐾 DO get to a hospital as fast as you can. Even if you don't immediately feel unwell, it is essential that you get medical treatment as quickly as possible. If the bite starts to swell up and changes colour, it means the snake that bit you was probably poisonous.

🐾 DO make a note of the exact time of the bite and of the size and appearance of the snake. This information will help the doctors who treat the bite. If possible, telephone the hospital with these details before you get there – that way they can have the correct treatment ready when you arrive.

If confronted by a snake stay calm and try and move slowly out of the snake's range. A snake will usually strike if it feels threatened, so don't do anything that might make it feel this way.

How To Avoid Lightning Strikes

You're walking to the shops on a sunny day and suddenly the sky darkens and a thunderstorm is unleashed. Follow this essential advice to stay safe:

* As soon as you see a flash of lightning, start counting. Count how many seconds it is before you hear the thunder (saying the word 'elephant' between each number you count will help you be more accurate). Take the number of seconds and divide it by three. This gives you a very approximate indication of how many kilometres away from you the storm is.

  If thunder follows the lightning by less than 20 seconds then you are near the centre of the storm and it is time to act.

* Avoid sheds, open-top cars, trees, flagpoles or mobile communication masts. If possible, get inside a large, enclosed building.

* Once inside, stay away from the telephone, water taps and electrical appliances such as the TV or computer. These items act as 'conductors' and

the lightning's electric charge can travel through them. If you touch a conductor that has been struck by lightning, the electric current produced will then flow into you. So stay well away from them!

If you can't get safely inside, and are in an exposed area such as a field or beach, here's what to do. Remove any metal objects, such as watches, rings or necklaces, and throw them away from you – these too can act as conductors. Kneel down, placing your fingers, knees and toes on the ground. Bend your head low to the ground and wait for the storm to pass.

How To Escape A Capsizing Ship

E ven the most sophisticated ships can be prone to peril at sea, especially in the North Atlantic where icebergs are rife and stormy waves can be huge. A big enough wave can cause even large ships to capsize, making them tip over and crash into the sea. If you're ever unlucky enough to find yourself in such danger and the captain of the ship gives the order, 'Abandon ship!', follow these instructions to maximize your chances of survival at sea.

PUT ON YOUR LIFE JACKET

A life jacket will keep you afloat in the water without any effort – this will save your body's energy which can be used to keep you warm instead. Try and cover up as much of your bare skin as possible before you put on your life jacket – this will help keep you warmer for longer.

If you don't have a life jacket, all is not lost. Your clothes will fill up with pockets of air, which will help to keep you floating, and also stop you from freezing.

CALMLY MOVE TO THE SHIP'S ASSEMBLY POINT

The assembly point is an area of the ship where passengers must gather in an emergency. You should be shown this area when you board a ship, but if you are not, always ask to see where this area is. Do not push or run when moving to an assembly point – this will only increase the panic levels and possibly cause injury among your fellow passengers.

WAIT FOR THE LIFE RAFTS TO BE RELEASED

Wait for your turn to descend. You will be hooked to a life line which descends over the open sea to the raft. Don't be tempted to jump into the sea without waiting for the life line – you might get swept away.

ROW, ROW, ROW

Once everyone is in the life rafts, the lines holding them to the ship will be cut. Everyone on board will need to row as hard as they can to get away from the ship. Remember, until you are clear, the ship could capsize on top of you at any moment or suck you under the water.

NO LIFE RAFTS

If there are no life rafts, throw something that will float into the water so that you can use it as a point to aim towards when you jump. If your life jacket is inflatable, wait until you leave the ship to inflate it, as you could cause yourself serious injury when you hit the water.

FLOAT FOR YOUR LIFE

If you are stranded in the sea waiting for the rescue boats to arrive, you will need to keep your energy up by using the floating survival technique.

FLOATING SURVIVAL TECHNIQUE

1. Stop swimming and let yourself float upright in the water.

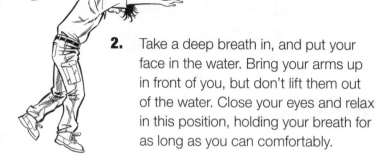

2. Take a deep breath in, and put your face in the water. Bring your arms up in front of you, but don't lift them out of the water. Close your eyes and relax in this position, holding your breath for as long as you can comfortably.

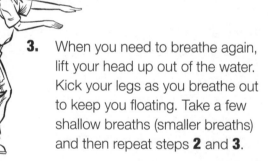

3. When you need to breathe again, lift your head up out of the water. Kick your legs as you breathe out to keep you floating. Take a few shallow breaths (smaller breaths) and then repeat steps **2** and **3**.

Swim as far away from the ship as possible and steer clear of any oil that might be leaking from the boat – it might catch fire. Swim slowly to keep your energy levels up.

How To Survive An Earthquake

The great majority of earthquakes are very slight. But stronger earthquakes can cause enormous damage.

1. If you are indoors, turn off all gas- and fire-related equipment. Take cover under a strong table and hold on to it. Alternatively, stand in a doorway. Keep clear of glass, fireplaces, heavy furniture and appliances. Stay put until the shaking stops and it's safe to move.

2. If you're outside, get out into the open. Stay away from buildings, trees, power lines, high walls and rocks.

3. If you're in a car, stay in the vehicle. Ask the driver to keep the car away from traffic, bridges, overpasses and tunnels, trees, lamp posts, power lines and road signs, and to stop the car where it seems safe.

4. After the shaking has stopped, check for injured people and make sure they're as comfortable as they can be. Check for hazards – fire, water leakages, damaged structures – turn off power supplies if a gas leak is suspected or electrical wiring is damaged. Only use the telephone for emergencies and keep listening to the radio. Expect aftershocks and even tidal waves.

The Richter Scale measures an earthquake's strength:

1–3	Generally not felt but recorded on seismographs (a piece of equipment that measure the motions of the ground)
3–4	Felt, but damage very rare
4–5	Widely felt, some local damage, not significant
5–6	Damage to poorly constructed buildings
6–7	Destructive – a fair amount of damage
7–8	Major – serious damage over large areas
8–9	Great – widespread destruction and loss of life
9 plus	Rare – causes great destruction over huge area

How To Defend A Medieval Castle

Defending a castle during medieval times wasn't easy. Attacks could be ruthless and you had to make do with the most basic of weapons. Good luck trying if you ever need to – here's a survival guide.

- ☙ If the attackers plan to break down the heavy wooden gates with a battering ram, like the one below, try pouring boiling water through holes floor of the battlements – called 'Murder Holes'.

🐾 Use the shape of the castle wall to your advantage. Castles are often built with a series of square holes, called 'crenellations', cut into the top walls. Defenders can shoot their arrows through these holes, and then retreat behind the cover of the wall. In the walls of the towers there are also thin windows, known as 'arrow loops', which are just the right size to shoot arrows through, but very difficult for the attackers down below to aim at.

🐾 Retreat into the 'keep' – that is the inner part of the castle. The keep is the safest place to be. Inside the keep there is enough food, water and provisions stored to keep you going for weeks.

How To Bust A Ghost

A true survivor is brave and fearless, but there are some adventures that are so scary, they will send chills down your spine. Dealing with ghosts is right at the top of that list (if you believe in them). While most ghosts mean you no harm, it's understandable that you don't want to be sharing your space with a spook.

You Will Need:

- a torch – in case the lights don't work
- a thermometer – a sudden drop in temperature could be a sign of a ghost
- a camera – if you see a ghost, take a picture for evidence
- a mobile phone – to record strange bumps in the night.

CHECKING FOR GHOSTS

Want to know if you are being haunted? Try these tricks.

☙ Hold a piece of string in your right hand, with your arm stretched out. Ask the ghost to give you a sign that it's nearby. If the string quivers, it may be your ghost showing its presence.

☙ Choose a fixed point and stare at it for 30 seconds. Relax your eyes, but keep looking at the fixed point. If you see a shadowy shape in the corner of your eye, chances are you have a ghost.

GHOST-BUSTING MOVES

Once you are sure you are being haunted, try these ancient ghost-busting tactics to get rid of your ghost for good.

☙ Walk to the centre of each room in your house, and in a loud, kind voice, say, 'It's time for you to move on, this is not the place for you.'

☙ Before you go to bed, put a pair of shoes at the end of your bed, pointing in different directions to each other. This is supposed to confuse a ghost and make it leave you alone.

☙ Sprinkle grains of rice on the floor each night. The spook will not be able to stop itself counting each grain. Having to do this every night for a week will give it such a headache that it will leave for good.

How To Make A Simple Raft

There may come a time when you have to take to the open sea, but find yourself without a vessel. Now is the time to learn how to make a raft. It may not be the most comfortable way to sail, but it could end up saving your life.

WARNING. Setting out into open water on a raft is very dangerous. Make sure it's your only option before attempting it.

You Will Need:

- 4 straight wooden poles, about 180cm long and 8–10cm thick
- 3 shorter wooden poles of the same thickness, but about 120cm long
- at least 61m of 5-mm thick nylon cord
- at least 12 strong 5-litre empty rectangular plastic containers of the kind used for detergent (caps should be screwed on tight)
- any planks or boards, at least 180cm long, that you can find
- nails
- a hammer
- a screwdriver
- scissors or a knife.

1. Lay the end of one of the shorter poles over the end of a longer one and at right angles to it, and lash them together with the nylon cord. Lay the other end of the shorter pole over the end of a second longer one, and lash together; then lash the free ends of the two longer poles under each end of a second shorter one – creating a rectangular structure.

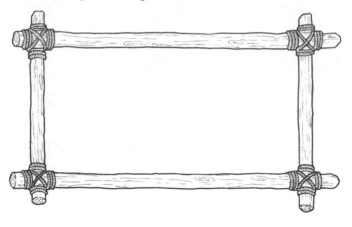

2. Lash each end of the third shorter pole across and over the middle of the two longer ones; then lash the third and fourth long poles beneath the middle of the three shorter crossways poles – the distance between these two long poles should be just wider than the narrowest side of one of the empty containers. You should now have a rectangle consisting of four long poles crossed by three shorter ones laid on top of them.

3. Now lash three of the empty 5-litre containers at even intervals along the outside of one of the outer long poles, the caps pointing towards the stern (rear) of the raft. Repeat along the outside of the other outer long pole, and then again between the two centre long poles.

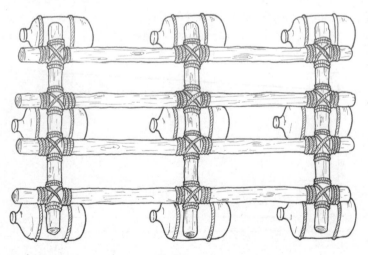

4. Launch the raft in shallow water and test its buoyancy – ideally, deck level should be about 15cm above the surface of the water when a person is sitting on the raft. If necessary, lash more containers to the long poles (you can get six containers along each pole) until you achieve the right degree of buoyancy. But remember to allow for the fact that you will be adding more weight when you fix the decking, which will make the raft sit lower in the water.

5. Now fix your decking of boards or planks to the three shorter cross poles – lash them in place, or otherwise nail or screw them to the cross poles. There can be gaps between the deck planks – in fact, the lighter you build your raft, the better it will float. The decking planks don't need to touch each other.

6. Relaunch the raft and climb aboard.

A useful knot for putting together a raft is the square lashing. You can find out how to do it by looking in a special knot book or a website dedicated to knot tying.

How To Make Your Escape

Even the most successful survivors can find themselves overwhelmed by enemy agents. Imagine you were captured by a rival organization and held against your will. How would you escape?

ESCAPE FROM A PAIR OF HANDCUFFS

Handcuffs are impossible to open, right? With the right tool, however, you can release them quite quickly. All you need is a simple, old-fashioned hairgrip. It is easy to hide one in the lining of a jacket or in a pocket, so make sure you have one within reach when you are captured. Try concealing it between your fingers or drop it on the floor within reach while you are being handcuffed. Then:

1. Once your captor has left the room, break the hairgrip so you can use the bendy section for grip and use the curved end for picking the lock.

2. Place the curved end into the keyhole on the cuffs, with the curve facing upwards. Make sure it's in the flat part of the keyhole, parallel with the handcuffs.

3. Apply steady pressure and push the grip forwards. The cuffs should spring open so that you can twist your hands out of them in one easy move.

ESCAPE FROM A LOCKED ROOM

Now you're free from any handcuffs or ropes, but how do you get past a locked door?

1. First, check to see if the key has been left in the lock. If it has, hunt around the room that you have been locked in for any useful equipment. Ideally, you'll be able to find a large sheet of paper and a pen or pencil.

2. Lay on the floor so that you can see through the gap between the door and the floor. Make sure that no one is around outside to see what you are up to. Keep an eye out for shadows approaching as you work.

3. Carefully and quietly, slide the piece of paper under the gap in the door, so that the largest portion of it is directly below the lock on the opposite side of the door.

4. Use the pen or pencil, or the hair grip if you still have it, to gently push the key out of the lock from your side of the door. As long as you don't push it too hard, the key should land on the piece of paper.

5. Pull the piece of paper slowly back towards you under the door, grab the key and make your escape.

How To
Survive
A Tornado

Tornadoes are windstorms that create a destructive, whirling funnel of air. They cause devastating damage to the areas they hit and happen with little warning.

PREPARATION

☙ The best way to survive a tornado is to be prepared for it. If you live in an area that is prone to tornadoes, keep an eye on the weather by regularly logging on to a weather website, or tuning into TV or radio weather forecasts.

☙ Keep a 'tornado kit' in a metal box inside your house. The kit should include a mobile phone, a portable radio, first-aid supplies, a bell, horn or whistle for signalling, and a flashlight.

☙ Additional supplies should include food, water, batteries and protective clothing. Keep your kit somewhere handy so you can grab it easily.

EARLY WARNING SIGNS

Here are some signs that you can look out for that will tell you if a twister is heading your way.

☙ Often you will hear a tornado coming before you see it. Listen out for a sound like a waterfall that turns into a roar as it gets closer. The sound of a tornado has been compared to that of a train or even a jet engine.

* The sky often turns a sickly greenish or greenish-black colour just before a storm hits.

* It may suddenly start to hail.

* You may notice clouds that are moving very fast, perhaps twisting into a cone shape.

* You might see debris, such as dust, branches and leaves, dropping from the sky.

* When the tornado arrives, you can expect to see a funnel-shaped cloud that is spinning rapidly. Debris will be pulled upwards into the funnel.

GET INSIDE

* The best place to be when a tornado arrives is inside. Houses in areas that are prone to tornadoes often have 'storm cellars' underneath them. These are the safest places to hide. If the building you're in does not have a cellar, head for the lowest floor. Find the smallest room on that floor, such as a bathroom or cupboard. If that's not possible, look for a room in the middle of the house with no windows. A hallway may provide the best shelter.

* Close any doors and windows that are located on the same side of the room as the approaching tornado. Open all the doors and windows

on the other side of the room. This will help prevent the powerful wind from entering the building. Tornadoes have been known to pick up entire buildings.

☙ Take shelter under some solid furniture, such as a heavy kitchen table. If you are in a bathroom jump into the bathtub. Cover yourself with a mattress, a sofa, towels or anything soft that you can get your hands on to protect yourself from flying debris.

SURVIVING OUTSIDE

☙ If you are unlucky enough to be caught outside without buildings nearby, try to get out of the path of the tornado by moving to the side, rather than trying to outrun it.

☙ If the only shelter you can find is in a ditch or hollow, make sure you lie face down and use your arms to protect your head and neck.

> **WARNING.** Never hide behind a tree or climb into a car, caravan or tractor, as these may be sucked up by the tornado.

How To Survive A Zombie Invasion

A zombie attack is probably the hardest challenge you will face. Zombies (or the 'undead', as they prefer to be known) are notoriously difficult to kill because they are not actually alive. As soon as you hear reports of zombies in your area, follow this plan of action.

GAME PLAN

* Gather as many survivors of the invasion as you can – there is safety in numbers. Find yourselves a secure building to use as a base. Ideally it should be on high ground. This will offer an excellent vantage point from which you can spot zombie hordes approaching, and the undead can't climb because their knees don't bend. Stock plenty of food and water – you may be surrounded by the undead for days.

🐾 Make sure the building has only two entrances (you need a second exit to escape through if zombies break through the front entrance). Build a barricade at each entrance and seal any other doors and windows with heavy furniture.

🐾 If someone has been infected you must get them out of your safe house quickly. The good news is once they are a full-blown zombie they won't feel pain and they'll never be forced to do anything they don't want to again, such as be nice to their granny. The bad news is they'll stink and their flesh will fall off.

HOW TO SPOT A ZOMBIE

🐾 The living dead are easy to spot because, as their name suggests, they are dead people whose bodies have come alive again. Look out for staring eyes, green skin and a pungent smell of rotting and decay. Check for a distinctive way of walking – slowly stumbling, with arms held straight out in front and a limp caused by their stiff knees.

🐾 If survivors come to your base asking for shelter – beware. They may have been infected. This happens if they are bitten or scratched by a zombie. There is no cure. They will become zombies too. Check all newcomers for any wounds.

BATTLING WITH THE UNDEAD

After a while you may get bored of waiting it out in barricaded base. Television broadcasts will eventually stop and there will be nothing but the sound of static on the radio. You may decide to venture outside. Be very careful.

🐾 Whenever you leave the shelter to gather fresh supplies or check for more survivors, carry a bat or sword to defend yourself. Guns are useless against zombies.

🐾 If you find yourself caught in a crowd of the undead, your best chance of surviving is to act like a zombie. Moan and keep your eyes as wide open as possible. Limp and dribble. Zombies are pretty stupid and with any luck they won't notice you among them.

🐾 Stay as fit and healthy as you can. Zombies are typically slow moving, but you never know when you'll need to outrun a speedy one.

🐾 If you're desperate, you can knock a zombie's head off and stop it in its tracks.

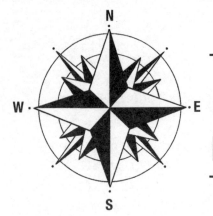

How To Get Home Using Nature's Clues

It's always a great idea to have a compass on you when out adventuring. But if your compass breaks or gets lost, you'll need to know how to use nature's clues to navigate your way home.

NORTH KNOW-HOW

The easiest way of working out where you are is to use the sun in the sky. If you are in the northern hemisphere (the half of the globe that is above the line of the equator), at 12 noon the sun is due south, and if you are in the southern hemisphere (the half of the globe below the line of the equator), it is due north.

Whichever hemisphere you are lost in, follow these instructions to find north using only a wristwatch:

🐾 To find north in the southern hemisphere, point 12 o'clock on the watch at the sun. Now find the middle point between 12 o'clock and the hour hand. This is north.

☙ In the northern hemisphere, you'll need to find south first. To do this, point the hour hand at the sun. Find the middle point between the hour hand and 12 o'clock. This is south, so the opposite direction is north.

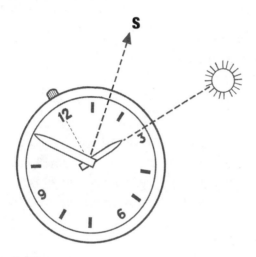

SUNSHINE CLUES

If you don't have a watch, don't worry – you can still work out which way is north by looking around you. Follow these clues to find north and south in the northern hemisphere (the opposite of each clue is true if you are lost in the southern hemisphere).

☙ Trees can be a useful guide. The side of the tree that faces south will have greater growth, as it will be getting more sunlight. There will be more branches growing horizontally on the southern side, and more branches growing vertically on the northern side.

🐾 The flowers of plants tend to face the sun – south.

🐾 If you are crossing over a hill, the north side will be damper with dew because it gets less sun.

🐾 Keep an eye out for a very tall hill or mountain in the distance. If it has snow on the top, the snow will be thicker and more noticeable on the north side.

🐾 Research has shown that herds of cows tend to stand with their bodies along a north-south line when they are resting or grazing on grass. The direction that their heads are facing is north.

POLE POSITION

Whichever side of the equator you are on, you can use this navigation technique to find north. All you need is a stick and a pebble.

1. Put a long stick in the ground so that it stands upright. The stick will cast a shadow. Put a small pebble (**A**) at the tip of the shadow.

2. Wait for roughly 20 minutes until another shadow is cast.

3. Place another pebble (**B**) at the end of the shadow that is now being made by the stick.

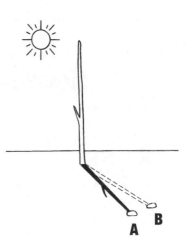

4. Next, make a mark midway between pebble **A** (which is in the west) and pebble **B** (in the east).

5. The line which runs from the base of your upright stick to the midpoint you have marked is called the north-south line. The direction of this line as it points away from your upright stick shows you which way is north.

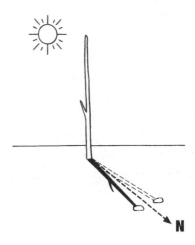

If you are lost at night time, you can navigate using the North Star. For instructions on how to do this, turn to page 61.

HOW TO CARRY
SOMEONE TO SAFETY

If someone in your expedition team has sprained their ankle but is still conscious and can hold themselves upright, you can make a stable seat with your hands simply by joining forces with another person.

1. Following the picture shown above, place your right hand on your left wrist, and grip tightly. Ask your lifting partner to do the same.

2. Now grip their right wrist with your left hand and get them to grip your right wrist. (As in the picture above.)

3. Lower the seat by both of you bending your legs, not your backs.

4. Get your casualty to sit on the four-handed seat and place his or her arms around both of the lifters' shoulders tightly.

5. When the casualty is seated, stand up, making sure you keep your back straight.

6. As soon as you have carried your casualty to safety, find a trained medical person who can examine them.

SAFETY POINTS

🐾 Do not lift anyone that may have a serious injury unless it is absolutely necessary. For example, if they face oncoming danger, such as a fire.

🐾 Always ask someone else for help when lifting. Don't try to lift a casualty on your own or you could end up dropping them and doing them more damage.

How To Survive The Bubonic Plague

I n the unlikely event that you wake up in medieval or
Elizabethan England, and discover that an epidemic of
the bubonic plague has reached your town or village, here
are some tips on how to survive it.

SURVIVAL STRATEGIES

🐾 Symptoms of the plague include a headache,
   aching joints, a fever and vomiting. Large lumps
   will appear around your armpits, neck and groin
   area, and black spots will appear on your skin.
   These are the 'buboes' from which the plague

takes its name. Watch out for these symptoms in yourself and your family.

🐾 Keep your house clean. By dropping food crumbs on the floor of your kitchen you may attract rats with fleas that are carrying the bubonic plague.

🐾 Don't copy your ancestors and carry flowers around with you because you think they will stop you getting the plague. They might cover up the smell of rotting plague victims, but they certainly won't stop you catching the dreaded disease.

COPING WITH THE CONTAGION

🐾 Shut yourself away in your house, but get word to anyone who has been near you that you have the plague, so they can get some medical help.

🐾 Do not stop bathing. It is essential that you keep your sores really clean so they are less likely to become infected.

🐾 Paint a red cross on your door. This will tell your friends that your household has become infected with the plague and they will know not to visit you after school.

🐾 Alternatively, you could try and survive until the 20th century when antibiotics will be available and your chances of survival will be much greater.

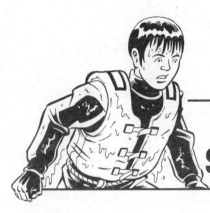

How To Survive At Sea

If you're sailing the crest of a wave, when suddenly your boat begins to sink, the gently-lapping sea will instantly becomes a treacherous ocean. In order to survive you are going to need skill, endurance – and the following tips.

STAY ON BOARD

You're more likely to survive at sea on a boat than on a life raft, so don't rush to abandon ship. Even if your boat is damaged, you're almost certainly better off on board. Why? Because the bigger the boat, the more visible it will be to a rescue party, and the better protected you are from the wind, water and sun.

PROPER PROVISIONS

If you have to leave your boat because it sinks, then your life raft should be equipped with a basic survival kit. This will include a short-wave radio, a GPS receiver (a Global Positioning System receiver which can calculate your exact position in the ocean), a compass, a knife, self-igniting flares, a waterproof watch, a waterproof torch, warm blankets, a box of matches in a waterproof container, a first-aid kit and some dry food. However, the most important thing you should have on board is fresh water. A lack of fresh, clean water will dramatically reduce the number of days you can stay alive.

WARNING. No matter how thirsty you get, NEVER be tempted to drink sea water. Sea water is three times as salty as your blood and your body would not be able to cope. It would also make you extremely thirsty.

You will also need to eat. There should be provisions in your raft, but once these are used up, don't panic. Fish should be plentiful in the ocean and flying fish may even land in your raft. If you don't have a fishing rod then try using twine and hooks made from wire or aluminium cans.

You can eat the flesh of fish raw. Don't forget to eat the eyes as well. Gross, but these contain water, too. Make sure you don't eat the organs or you may become sick.

STAY DRY

Sea water is your number one enemy, so your main aim should be to keep dry and stay warm. If you are out in cold weather, you could develop 'hypothermia' (a condition that sets in when your body temperature drops below its normal level). This can kill within a short space of time. If you're in hot weather, exposure to sea water and sun can damage your skin, leading to blisters and other infections.

So if your life raft has a canopy, use it. If not, try to rig up sheets and blankets as a shelter from the waves and from the sun as soon as possible. If you remain exposed, you will survive for a shorter time than if you are under cover.

STAY OR GO?

Even if you know your location, attempting to row towards land may not be your best strategy. Currents and riptides may push you further from your destination and your efforts to row the life raft may waste precious energy.

If your boat was able to send a distress signal before it sank, staying close to where you sent the flare will mean that you are more likely to be found by potential rescuers.

SIGNAL AND SURVIVE

A survivor in a life raft will be almost invisible in the vast seascape. As a result, it's vital you are ready to signal to any passing plane or ship. If you have self-igniting flares and a short-wave radio then make sure you know how to use them so you are ready to swing into action at any time.

If you don't have either device, use a hand-held mirror to reflect sunlight towards rescuers, or attract attention by using a whistle or a torch. As a last resort, waving brightly coloured material may also be effective.

WARNING. Before setting out on a voyage, always tell someone your route and the time you will arrive at your destination. This way people will know where to look if you don't arrive.

How To Survive
An Arctic Adventure

The Arctic regions can experience terrifying storms, and temperatures as low as minus 80°C. Amazingly, though, people do live in these areas. The Inuit people,

who make the Arctic their home, are experts in survival skills. If you're ever trekking towards the North Pole and a blizzard begins, you can build yourself a snow hole to shelter in until the storm passes.

HOW TO BUILD A SNOW HOLE

1. Find a large slope of snow in which to dig your shelter. Slopes of snow are easier to tunnel into.

2. Using a shovel, dig a tunnel, about one metre in length, into the side of the slope.

3. Scrape away an area of snow at the end of your tunnel. Continue to scrape out snow until you have made a hole large enough for you to crawl into. Stop scraping when your snow hole is big enough for you to fit yourself and your equipment inside, and tall enough for you to sit up in.

WARNING. Keep the roof of your snow hole as thick as possible – a thick roof will keep your hole warm and also minimize the danger of your snow hole caving in on top of you.

4. Before climbing into your snow hole, spike the ends of your ski poles into the roof. This way, other explorers can spot your shelter and find you easily if they need to.

5. Inside your snow hole, use some of the snow that you scraped away to create a ledge by patting this snow down above the floor of your shelter. Cold air is heavier than warm air and will collect near the floor of your shelter, so having a ledge to sit on will help keep you warm.

6. Put all your belongings in the snow hole, and position something bulky (like your rucksack) in the entrance to keep out some of the cold air.

7. Using a twig or a stick, carefully make three holes in the top of your shelter for ventilation. This way you can safely burn candles inside your snow hole, or light a small camping stove to give you extra warmth.

8. Smooth over the walls and roof inside your snow hole. Your body heat will warm up the snow around you and smoothing the snow on the walls should stop drips.

Now you can shelter from the blizzard in comfort, before heading off on your adventure again.

How To Avoid Being Chomped By A Hippo

If you think hippos are chilled-out mud-wallowers, think again – they can be very aggressive. They are huge animals, weighing as much as four tonnes, with razor-sharp tusk-like teeth. Hippos have even been known to bite crocodiles in half. Bearing this in mind, you might want to stay away from hippo habitats, but here are a few tips just in case:

EMERGENCY TACTICS

* Keep as far away from the hippo as you can. There are two types of hippo to avoid particularly – female hippos protecting their young and hungry hippos short of food during a drought.

* If a hippo opens its vast jaws, it's probably not yawning – the animal is showing you that it has

very big teeth and could attack at any moment. Make sure you heed this aggressive warning.

🐾 Show that you're not a threat by backing away slowly. If the hippo sees that you're moving out of its territory by yourself, it might not feel the need to help you on your way.

🐾 Try and make sure you're downwind of the hippo, so that the wind isn't carrying your scent straight up the hippo's nostrils, and sending angry messages to its brain.

🐾 Never block a hippo's path to water. This is guaranteed to make it cross.

🐾 Running away won't do you much good, because a hippo will easily outrun you. As a last resort, run as fast as you can to the nearest tree, climb it and shout for help.

How To Survive
A Swarm Of
Angry Honeybees

A bee may sting you if it feels threatened. Honeybees die after they sting, so they avoid it if possible. But don't be fooled, bee venom packs a punch, and multiple bee stings are very dangerous and can be fatal. When bees swarm they can be very aggressive and will try to defend their hive at all costs. Here are some tips about what to do if you encounter a swarm.

GOOD IDEAS

* Put as much distance as you can between you and the hive. The bees will pursue and sting you until they no longer see you as a threat.

* Take cover, in a building if possible, and shut all the doors and windows. If you can't, run through

long grass or scrubland, which should give you
some cover.

BAD IDEAS

* Don't approach a hive.

* Don't swat the bees. It will make them sting you.

* Don't attempt to escape by getting into water.
  They may wait above the water for you to surface.

DEALING WITH STINGS

* A honeybee will leave its stinger in you. Gently
  scrape this out with your fingernail as soon as you
  can to stop it injecting more venom.

* Apply a cold compress to relieve the pain and
  swelling. Alternatively, apply a substance called
  'meat tenderizer' (such as papain) to the sting.
  This will break down the bee's venom.

* If you have received more than a dozen stings, or
  have been stung in or around your mouth or nose,
  seek medical help immediately.

WARNING. If you are allergic to
bee venom and get stung, seek
immediate medical attention.

How To Survive A Rip Current

A rip current is an area of water near the surface of the sea that is flowing rapidly away from shore. Rip currents can pull even the strongest swimmers out to sea. However, once you know how to deal with rip currents, you should be able to get back to shore safely.

EMERGENCY TACTICS

* If you are swimming and suddenly realize you are being pulled out to sea by a current, don't panic! Panicking will only make you disoriented – you need to keep a clear head. You have a very good chance of getting back to shore, and the current won't drag you under the water.

* Don't try and swim back to shore. You won't be strong enough to swim against the current, and trying to do so will just tire you out. Swim parallel with the line of the beach.

☙ If the pull of the current makes this too difficult, just wait until the current takes you into an area of calmer water.

☙ Rip currents are usually no more than about ten metres wide. Once you've swum far enough along, parallel to the beach, you should arrive outside the area affected by the current. Then you should be able to swim back in to shore, or you can let the waves take you back in.

☙ On tourist beaches there are usually signs warning you if the area is prone to dangerous rip currents. Take notice of these warnings and never swim in areas that are marked as unsafe. Always stick to the area of the beach that is patrolled by a trained lifeguard.

WARNING. Don't go into the sea on your own, and if you're not a strong swimmer, stay in shallow water.

How To Throw An Opponent

If an opponent rushes you from behind, here is a basic self-defence technique that will help you use your opponent's attack to your advantage.

WARNING. Never practise this move on an unsuspecting opponent and always make sure that there are plenty of soft mattresses or mats around to provide a soft landing while you are practising.

WHAT YOU DO

Practise this manoeuvre with a friend, taking turns to be the attacker and to defend yourself. Use a mat to break your fall.

1. It's important to act quickly, so as soon as you feel your opponent's hand grab you, grip his arm firmly with both hands.

2. Rather than trying to pull his arm away from you, tug it forwards and downwards – this is much easier to do.

3. Take a large step forward, bringing your opponent with you. This will not only take him by surprise, but will also throw him off balance.

4. Without pausing, bend your knees into a crouching position and lean forwards at the waist.

5. As your opponent begins falling forwards, tilt your body to the side and use his momentum to pull him forwards, landing him on his back on the mat.

How To Find Your Way In A Maze

Mazes are the perfect place for an enemy to trap you. If you ever get stuck in a maze and time is of the essence to escape quickly, then you will need to know these clever tricks to find your way to freedom.

A-MAZE-ING SOLUTIONS

One of the most famous mythical mazes in history was escaped from using a ball of thread. According to Greek legend, King Minos built a huge maze to contain a savage beast called a Minotaur (a terrifying creature with a human body and the head of a bull).

One day, a young man called Theseus decided to defeat the Minotaur. When the King's daughter, fell in love with Theseus, she said she would help him and gave him a ball of thread. Before Theseus entered the maze, he tied the end of the thread to the entrance and let it unwind as he made his way through and killed the sleeping Minotaur. Following the thread back, he found his way back to the entrance and escaped.

If you don't have any thread handy, here are more maze-solving tricks to try.

- As you enter the maze, mark arrows on the floor using chalk – follow these back to the entrance.

- If you go down a dead end, walk back to where you turned into it. Draw a line in the ground across the path so you know not to go down it again.

- If you keep your right hand touching the wall at all times as you walk, you will get to the centre and back again. However, this route will take you down a few dead ends.

How To Survive In Bear Country

As reluctant as they are to bump into you, unfortunately bears can't resist the smell of the food. So if you're hanging around in bear country, it's essential to avoid bears visiting your camp for lunch.

THE BEAR NECESSITIES

1. Never store food in your tent – keep it at least 50m from camp in bear-proof boxes. Alternatively, store your food in an airtight container, put it in a bag, and hang it from the branch of a tree.

2. Establish your cooking area at least 50m from camp. Always clean up thoroughly after eating. Burn or bury all leftover food well away from camp.

3. Never keep scented items or toiletries in your tent. Toothpaste and lip-balms are tasty treats for bears.

4. Don't burn 'citronella' candles (sold to keep insects away). Their scent has been known to attract bears.

5. Never put food out for bears in the hope you will spot one. They will only come looking for more food and might get angry when you can't give them any more.

6. When you are out and about, make plenty of noise. Any bears in the area will probably stay out of your way. Attach bells to your ankles or clap and sing as you hike.

BEAR BEWARE!

🐾 If a bear approaches, don't run or scream. Speak in a calm voice and back away with your head tilted downwards, but keep your eyes on the bear.

🐾 If a bear attacks, play dead. Roll on to your front and curl into a ball, clasping your hands behind your neck. Stay still until the bear loses interest. If it doesn't show signs of leaving you alone, or becomes ferocious, fight it off with all your might.

How To Survive In The Desert

The most important thing to do when you find yourself alone in the desert is to find shelter from the sun. Look for shadows cast by scrub vegetation or rocks. Shelter during the day and travel by night, when it is much cooler.

CONSTRUCT A SOLAR STILL

The biggest problem you will face is the lack of water. To ensure you have a source of water, construct a 'solar still'.

1. Take a plastic bag and cut down one side seam and along the bottom edge. Open it out so you have a large plastic sheet.

2. Dig a shallow hole.

3. In the middle of the hole place a cup upright in the sand, below the level of the ground.

4. Cover the hole with the plastic sheet and anchor it with stones around its edge. Place a small stone in the middle of the plastic so it is directly above the cup.

5. Water vapour will condense underneath the plastic sheet and drip into the cup.

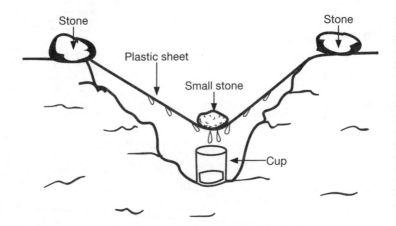

ESSENTIAL SURVIVAL TIPS

🐾 Your solar still will not provide much water, so you need to conserve your bodily fluids. The biggest cause of water loss is sweating. You need to keep your mouth closed and breathe through your nose.

This reduces the amount of water you lose from your body. Make sure your movements are slow and regular to keep your sweating to a minimum.

* Keep as much of your body covered as possible to protect your skin from the sun and hot winds. If you have a hat keep it on to protect you from sunstroke and to conserve moisture. If you don't have a hat tie a piece of cloth around your head. Make sure it hangs over the back of your neck.

* Watch out for signs that you are suffering from too much heat. You will start to feel very tired and disorientated.

* Check the colour of your wee. If it is dark browny yellow, you are dehydrated. The moment you are aware of any of these warning signs drink a few sips of water every hour.

* The large expanse of mostly empty terrain in deserts will cause you to underestimate distances. As a general rule, things are about three times further away than you think.

* Sandstorms are frequent in the desert. If you get caught in one, stay calm. Look for something to shelter behind. Cover your nose and mouth with clothing and lie down flat, with your back to the wind, until it has passed.

How To Survive An Alien Encounter

If you're lucky enough to meet an alien on one of your adventures, stick to the following advice to make sure your encounter is a safe one.

ALIEN ADVICE

- ❀ Aliens could look very different from humans, so be prepared to encounter tentacles, many eyes, fangs or slimy bodies. Never look shocked. It is vital that you don't offend an alien. You don't want it to use its laser gun on you! Keep your facial expressions neutral at all times.

- ❀ Aliens probably won't speak Earth languages, but they could have a gadget that can help them to translate any language. Make sure you speak slowly and repeat any long words to ensure they understand you.

- ❀ If an alien invites you to come on board its spacecraft, politely say no. There are stories about humans being abducted (kidnapped) by aliens, and even though these may not be true, you want to keep your adventures on this planet.

The alien may be very interested in you, so why not introduce it to some typical Earthling food? Whether you serve afternoon tea or a hamburger and chips, have lots of napkins handy – eating with tentacles is a tricky business, and you don't want the alien to feel embarrassed.

How To Cross A Rope Bridge

Faced with a fast-flowing stream while trekking on an adventure through the jungle, how will you make sure your team of adventurers and all the equipment make it to the other side without being swept away by the current?

As long as you've brought that most essential piece of adventurer's equipment – your trusty ropes – you can make a bridge that everyone can cross safely. Read on to learn how.

You Will Need:

- 2 long, strong ropes
- thick fabric (offcuts from an old carpet or mat is ideal)
- 2 trees, roughly 4m apart
- a tape measure.

1. If you are on a jungle adventure, find a point along the stream where there are two strong trees on either side.

2. Measure 50cm up from the base of the tree trunk, on the side of the stream that you are on. Tie some thick fabric around the tree at this point – this will protect the bark of the tree when you tie the rope to it.

3. Measure 1.5m up the tree (above the wrapped fabric) and tie some more thick fabric around the tree here.

4. Now you need to secure the ropes to the tree. To do this, tie one end of rope around the bottom of the tree, at the point where you have tied the fabric, using a knot called a clove hitch. Follow the steps below to learn how to do this:

HOW TO TIE A CLOVE HITCH KNOT

5. Wrap the rope once around the tree trunk, crossing one end of the rope (**A**) over the other rope end (**B**).

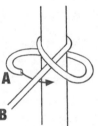

6. Wrap end **A** around the tree trunk again, making a second turn, and thread it under rope **B**, as shown.

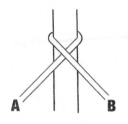

7. Thread rope **A** under the second turn. Pull the rope through and tighten. Pull on the ropes as hard as you can to make sure you have tied the knot correctly. This rope is for walking on.

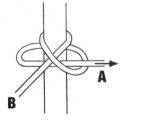
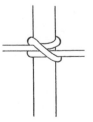

8. Now you need to tie the end of the second rope over the fabric that is higher up the tree. Repeat steps **5** to **7** to secure this end to the tree. This rope will be for holding on to while you are crossing the rope bridge.

9. Gather the ends of both ropes in large loops. Wade carefully across the stream to the other side, unwinding the ropes as you go.

10. Once you have successfully crossed the stream, tie the ends of each rope to the tree on this side of the stream, by repeating steps **2** to **8**.

It is very important the ropes are tied so they are not too slack. If the bottom rope is slack, it could dip into the stream when you stand on it. If the top rope is slack, it could cause you to tip over and fall in.

WARNING. Never wade through water that is deeper than your calf – strong currents may knock you off your feet.

CROSSING A ROPE BRIDGE

🐾 Stand on the bottom rope, holding the top rope, and shuffle sideways across the bridge.

🐾 If you have baggage to get across the stream, tie it to the top rope with a loop and pull it along to the other side.

🐾 Only ever cross a rope bridge one person at a time – if the rope breaks, you and your baggage will get very wet.

HOW TO ESCAPE THE CLUTCHES OF A BOA CONSTRICTOR

If you meet a boa constrictor on an adventure, the good news is that these snakes are not venomous. The bad news is that they can be over four metres long and over 30 kilograms in weight. They use their strong, powerful bodies to wrap themselves around their prey and suffocate it. They then open their huge jaws and enjoy a tasty feast. Read on to learn how to avoid becoming a snake's snack.

WHERE THEY LIVE
Boas live in the tropical regions of Central and South America. Although they live on dry land in hollow trees and logs, you may find one as you wade through rivers, as boas are very good swimmers.

FEEDING HABITS
A constrictor will eat anything it can catch and swallow, including birds, monkeys and even pigs. A boa only wraps itself around something it intends to eat. It does not think of humans as food because they are too big for it to swallow, so it is very rare that a boa will attempt to eat you.

SENSE OF SMELL

A boa will only wrap itself around you if it smells another animal's scent on you and becomes confused. To avoid being mistaken for something a boa could eat, wash your hands thoroughly after making your lunch in the jungle.

BOA BITES

The mouth of a constrictor is filled with tiny, hooked teeth which it uses to hold its prey down. If a boa is frightened it will defend itself by biting you. This is painful, but not fatal.

STAY STILL

If a boa does decide to attack you, don't struggle – this will only make it squeeze tighter. Shout to someone else in your group to pour some vinegar into its mouth as this might make it release you. It this fails, grab your pocket knife and cut off its head.

How To Make An Underwater Escape

In the movies, the hero always seems to be plunging his car into the water, where he inevitably makes an incredible escape. Here's how to do it for real.

IF THE CAR FLOATS ...

* You are not doomed. Most cars will float for a while, giving you time to save the day. Immediately remove your seatbelt so you are ready for action.

* As soon as your car enters the water, release the door locks. If you can, open the doors before the car begins to sink and use them to escape. You won't be able to open the doors once the car is partially submerged, because the weight of the water is pushing against them.

* If the doors won't open, wind down your windows as quickly as possible. Electric windows should still work while your car is afloat, but will stop working as soon as the mechanism or the car's battery is submerged. Climb out of a window and swim to safety.

If you are unable to open your doors or windows, try to smash a window. Use something heavy like a wrench, or the metal end of a headrest. Smash it at the corner as this is where the window is weakest.

IF THE CAR SINKS ...

* If the car sinks before you can do any of the above, you are going to have to wait until the car has filled with water. This will equalize the pressure of the water inside and outside the car.

* Climb into the back seat because the front of the car, where the heavy engine is, will sink first.

* Wait until the water has reached neck height. Then instruct everyone to take a big gulp of air.

* Once the doors are completely submerged, they should open with a push. Try shoving a door with your feet while steadying yourself by grabbing on to a seat. Exit the car, and swim away and up to the surface.

HOW TO MAKE A CAMP IN THE WILDERNESS

If your plane crashes in the middle of nowhere, you'll need to keep yourself alive until help arrives. You can survive for much longer without food than without water, so finding water is your first priority. You'll need to find a spot to set up camp that is near a source of water, but not too near, as wild animals may gather there to drink.

BUILDING A CAMP

🐾 You need to build a lean-to to keep you dry and protected from the elements. See if you can find a fallen tree, a natural cave or a big rock to build your lean-to against.

🐾 Collect thick sticks and branches and prop them up at an angle along the tree trunk or rock face. Make sure the space under the line of sticks is long enough to cover your whole body.

🐾 Gather smaller branches and sticks, and use them to fill the gaps between the larger ones, then heap leaves, grass, moss or ferns over the sticks. This will keep some of the wind and rain out of your lean-to.

🐾 You can find more details on this type of shelter and instructions on how to build another type of shelter on page 20.

🐾 Collect a large stack of dry wood to make a fire. You can also use bark or dry animal dung.

🐾 It's a good idea to make your fire at least ten paces from your lean-to, as you don't want the dry brush to catch fire.

🐾 To keep yourself extra warm at night, you could heat rocks on the fire and then bury them in the ground and sleep on top of them.

- ❧ It is essential to keep your fire alight at all times and have a pile of damp leaves ready beside it. If you hear a plane or helicopter fly overhead, throw the leaves on top of the fire to create a plume of smoke that will attract attention.

- ❧ When it comes to foraging for food, be careful. Don't be tempted by mushrooms – even experts sometimes find it hard to tell which ones are good to eat and which are poisonous.

- ❧ Berries can also be dangerous. As a general rule, most white or yellow berries are poisonous and most blue or black berries are not, but there are exceptions.

- ❧ Your best bet is to eat insects. It may sound disgusting, but they are nutritious and are not likely to be harmful.

It is better to stay in one place if you know someone will be looking for you, otherwise you may just be moving around and missing each other.

How To Read A Compass

K nowing how to read a compass is a must when trying to navigate your way from A to B. A compass uses magnetic dials to locate the magnetic north pole.

1. Hold the compass out flat so that the needle can spin around freely.

2. Stand still for a few moments until the north-seeking end of the needle (usually marked with red paint) settles in one position – this is magnetic north.

3. Keep the compass level and turn the dial until the orienting mark for north is over the coloured end of the needle. Now you know exactly which way south, east and west are, too.

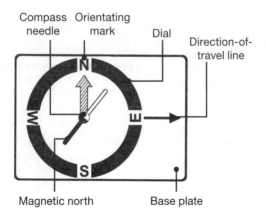

Compass needle   Orientating mark   Dial   Direction-of-travel line   Magnetic north   Base plate

How To Put Out The Great Fire Of London

The Great Fire of London was a fire that swept through London from 2nd September to 5th September 1666. It consumed 13,200 houses, 87 churches and even St Paul's Cathedral. If you'd like to have had a go at extinguishing this blaze, here's how you might have survived it.

FIGHTING FIRE

* You could have used axes, ropes and hooks to pull down a row of houses to make large gaps in the buildings that the fire couldn't leap across. But

fire is fast stuff, and can sometimes jump gaps as quickly as they are made.

☙ In 1666 there was no fire brigade. You would have had to employ teamwork to survive, by lining the streets with people, and passing buckets of water from hand to hand – which would have been tremendously slow work. There was something called a 'fire squirt' which pumped water, but it was about as much use as a giant water pistol.

☙ London did have fire engines at this time, but they proved rather useless. Only some of them had wheels, while others were mounted on wheelless sleds. You would have had to drag them a long way through the crowded streets and even then would have suffered a severe lack of water with which to use them. The fire would have spread too rapidly for such a slow tactic to work, endangering everybody's lives.

☙ You might have used gunpowder to blast rows of houses out of the way to stop the fire spreading. This was much faster than pulling them down with only ropes and hooks. If you'd have been brave enough to put yourself in such danger, it would have worked, as this was eventually what finally put the fire out.

HOW TO MAKE A SWIFT EXIT

Whether or not you're ever in a situation where you need to limbo dance to freedom, why not practise this life-saving skill by holding a limbo competition with your friends?

You Will Need:
- 3 or more friends
- 2 bamboo canes
  (at least 1m long)
- a tape measure
- a pen.

1. On one cane, mark a point 60cm from one end using your pen. Measure 10cm sections from that point until you reach 1m, making a mark each time. This is your measuring cane.

2. Ask two friends to hold the other cane at each end, around 1m high, parallel to the ground. (Use your measuring cane as a guide.)

3. Take it in turns to limbo under the cane. To do this, spread your legs shoulder-width apart and stretch your arms out on either side of your body. Take small steps forwards towards the cane, bending your knees and leaning backwards as you move. Don't lean back too far – you will lose your balance and fall over. If a player's body touches the cane, or their hands touch the ground, they are out.

4. Lower the cane by 10cm so that it is now 90cm off the ground – in line with the mark on your measuring cane. Players must now try to limbo under it again.

5. Continue lowering the cane by 10cm, making it harder to limbo underneath it. The player that can limbo the lowest, wins.

How To Survive A Flood

If you live or are holidaying in an area that is coastal or low-lying, with a history of flooding, a flood could potentially happen at any time. It is vital that you are prepared.

EMERGENCY KIT

Keep an emergency kit close at hand, stored somewhere that is accessible and above floodwater levels. Your emergency kit should be sealed in a waterproof container and should include:

- drinking water in sealed bottles
- a medical kit
- maps of the area
- signalling devices (including a torch and a mobile phone)
- a spare set of clothes
- a sleeping bag or blankets
- sealed plastic wallets to keep your passport and any other important documents safe.

PREPARATION

- ❧ Advance notice of a flood or approaching tidal wave could mean the difference between life and death, so make sure you follow news bulletins on the radio and TV.

- On the first day of a holiday you should familiarize yourself with the area in which you are staying. You need to establish a prearranged meeting place on high ground or in a tall, well-constructed building. Make sure that all the members of your family know a route out of the holiday complex that will take them to your prearranged meeting place, avoiding low-lying areas, that may flood.

- If possible, make sure everyone in your group carries a mobile phone at all times and that they have the number for everyone else in the group and for the emergency services.

TIME TO GO

- If you are lucky enough to have advance warning of a flood, you must prepare to leave your house. Turn off all gas and electrical appliances at the mains.

- Large objects carried in flood waters are a danger to you and other people, so lock your family's car inside the garage and bolt the door. Tie down any objects you can to stop them floating away.

- Grab your emergency kit and start to make your way to your meeting place.

☙ Never try to outrun a flood by jumping in a car and speeding off. The floodwater will move faster than you can.

☙ Don't be tempted to cross a torrent of water that looks shallow. It is dangerous to wade through water that is any deeper than your knees. Moreover, it is very difficult to tell how strong the current is just by looking at it. The pressure of fast-flowing water on your legs can easily make you lose your balance and fall.

☙ If you do get swept up in floodwater, try to grab something you can climb on to. While you are in the water you are at risk of being struck by debris being carried by the flood. Another potential danger in some areas of the world can be wildlife, such as snakes and crocodiles, which may be swept along in the waters, too.

HIGHER GROUND

☙ Once you reach your meeting place, use your phone to make your position known to the emergency services. Make sure everyone with you understands how important it is to stay there until help comes.

☙ While you wait, ration the food and water you have with you among the people you are sheltering with. Do not allow anyone to be tempted to drink from the floodwater. It will be contaminated and will probably make them sick. Use your first-aid kit to tend to anyone injured.

If you have enough time before leaving your home, move furniture and valuables upstairs.

HOW TO SURVIVE IN A HORROR MOVIE

Horror movies are just made up, right? Well, probably, but you can never be too careful. As it's probably the most unexpected dangerous situation to be confronted with, you'll need to be extra prepared.

THE DOS AND DON'TS OF HORROR MOVIES

🐾 When it appears that you have killed a monster, DON'T approach it to check if it's really dead – it will pounce on you.

🐾 DO watch your step. When running away from a monster expect to fall over at least twice.

🐾 DON'T accept invitations from strangers who live in isolated areas and have no contact with society – no matter how innocent they seem.

🐾 If your car breaks down at night, DON'T go to a deserted-looking mansion to phone for help. Always keep your mobile charged up or use a payphone.

🐾 DO stay with your friends. It's never a good idea to venture out on your own.

🐾 DON'T search the basement – especially if the lights have just gone out and the phone is dead.

🐾 If you discover any of your friends have fangs, DON'T invite them round.

🐾 If any of your friends' skin starts to turn green and rot, DON'T go round to their house – they'll most likely try to eat your brains.

🐾 DON'T ever say 'I'll be right back.' You won't be.

How To Build An Igloo

Cold temperatures can be deadly. When your body temperature drops below normal, it won't take long for hypothermia to set in. If you are ever on an expedition in the polar regions, it won't hurt to learn how to build an igloo to keep yourself safe and warm.

1. Use a stick to mark a circle in the snow about 3.5m across. Grab a snow shovel and dig out the circle to a depth of about 15cm. Trample down the circle of snow with your feet.

2. Find a large, clear area of deep snow near by and jump on it until it is flat. This is going to be your snow quarry.

3. Use your shovel to cut out some snow bricks about 70cm long, 50cm wide and 20cm deep.

4. Build a layer of snow bricks around the outside of your circle. Shape the bricks so that the row makes a spiral shape. (Leave a gap for the entrance.) Get a friend to work from the inside of the igloo, filling in the cracks with snow.

5. Build a second layer of bricks, cutting each brick so that they continue to make a spiral. Then create more layers of bricks until you have an igloo shape with a hole at the top.

6. 'Cap' the hole with a single block of packed snow. Cut a block that is slightly bigger than the hole and get your partner to help lift it up and put it in place.

7. Climb inside the igloo and trim the cap so that it fits the hole. Pack snow around the edges of the cap.

8. Dig out a little trench from the snow leading up to the entrance hole.

9. Make an arch over your entrance hole by placing two narrow bricks either side. Make sure the arch will be big enough for you to crawl through easily.

10. Make a couple of small slits near the top and bottom of the igloo. These will allow air in and out.

WARNING. Keep your igloo-building skills for Arctic expeditions. Igloos can be dangerous if they collapse on top of you. So at home, stick to snuggling up in your own heated home. And if you must build an igloo in snowy territory, make sure you don't do it alone.

HOW TO TRACK ANIMALS

When surviving out in the wilderness, knowing how to track a wild animal will come in handy. But before you can track one, you must be able to recognize its footprints.

Here are some tracks you won't mind finding:

Dog   Cat   Fox   Badger   Running rabbit

Here are some tracks you should not follow:

Hyena   Bear   Hippo   Mountain lion

🐾 The best time to go tracking is early in the morning or late in the day. When the sun is low in the sky, tracks will be edged with shadow, making them more visible.

🐾 Take a tracking guidebook with you, so you can identify any unusual tracks you come across.

🐾 Scout around for tracks. Brush loose leaves and vegetation aside.

🐾 When you find a trail of prints, mark each one by pushing a stick into the ground next to it. This will help you to see the size of the animal's stride, and guess at how big the animals might be.

🐾 Use a magnifying glass to look closely at the prints. You might find an animal had a clipped hoof or damaged claw. This will help you distinguish it from other animals.

🐾 Look out for droppings, chewed plants and any other signs of animal activity.

🐾 Don't look down at your feet. You'll track down the animal much faster if you look between 5m and 10m away from your body

🐾 Stay low, move slowly and be as quiet as you can. Even the sound of a snapping twig could make your animal run off.

YOU WILL ALSO LOVE:

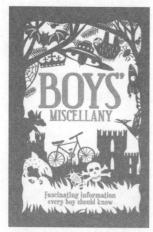

ISBN: 978-1-78055-040-4

ISBN: 978-1-78055-041-1

ISBN: 978-1-78055-194-4

ISBN: 978-1-78055-195-1